Markus Maucher

On the influence of non-perfect randomness on probabilistic algorithms

Markus Maucher

On the influence of non-perfect randomness on probabilistic algorithms

Südwestdeutscher Verlag für Hochschulschriften

Impressum/Imprint (nur für Deutschland/ only for Germany)
Bibliografische Information der Deutschen Nationalbibliothek: Die Deutsche Nationalbibliothek verzeichnet diese Publikation in der Deutschen Nationalbibliografie; detaillierte bibliografische Daten sind im Internet über http://dnb.d-nb.de abrufbar.

Alle in diesem Buch genannten Marken und Produktnamen unterliegen warenzeichen-, marken- oder patentrechtlichem Schutz bzw. sind Warenzeichen oder eingetragene Warenzeichen der jeweiligen Inhaber. Die Wiedergabe von Marken, Produktnamen, Gebrauchsnamen, Handelsnamen, Warenbezeichnungen u.s.w. in diesem Werk berechtigt auch ohne besondere Kennzeichnung nicht zu der Annahme, dass solche Namen im Sinne der Warenzeichen- und Markenschutzgesetzgebung als frei zu betrachten wären und daher von jedermann benutzt werden dürften.

Verlag: Südwestdeutscher Verlag für Hochschulschriften Aktiengesellschaft & Co. KG
Dudweiler Landstr. 99, 66123 Saarbrücken, Deutschland
Telefon +49 681 37 20 271-1, Telefax +49 681 37 20 271-0
Email: info@svh-verlag.de
Zugl.: Ulm, Universität, Diss., 2009

Herstellung in Deutschland:
Schaltungsdienst Lange o.H.G., Berlin
Books on Demand GmbH, Norderstedt
Reha GmbH, Saarbrücken
Amazon Distribution GmbH, Leipzig
ISBN: 978-3-8381-1231-2

Imprint (only for USA, GB)
Bibliographic information published by the Deutsche Nationalbibliothek: The Deutsche Nationalbibliothek lists this publication in the Deutsche Nationalbibliografie; detailed bibliographic data are available in the Internet at http://dnb.d-nb.de.

Any brand names and product names mentioned in this book are subject to trademark, brand or patent protection and are trademarks or registered trademarks of their respective holders. The use of brand names, product names, common names, trade names, product descriptions etc. even without a particular marking in this works is in no way to be construed to mean that such names may be regarded as unrestricted in respect of trademark and brand protection legislation and could thus be used by anyone.

Publisher: Südwestdeutscher Verlag für Hochschulschriften Aktiengesellschaft & Co. KG
Dudweiler Landstr. 99, 66123 Saarbrücken, Germany
Phone +49 681 37 20 271-1, Fax +49 681 37 20 271-0
Email: info@svh-verlag.de

Printed in the U.S.A.
Printed in the U.K. by (see last page)
ISBN: 978-3-8381-1231-2

Copyright © 2010 by the author and Südwestdeutscher Verlag für Hochschulschriften Aktiengesellschaft & Co. KG and licensors
All rights reserved. Saarbrücken 2010

Acknowledgements

The work in this thesis was supported by grants to Uwe Schöning (DFG) and Hans A. Kestler (BMBF NGFNplus). I am very indebted for that financial support. I also gratefully thank the bwGRiD project [1] for the computational resources. Most of our experiments were run on that grid.

I am also indebted to my colleagues at the University of Ulm, both in the Theoretical Computer Science group as well as in the Applied Bioinformatics group. Thank you very much for the many fruitful discussions. Special thanks to Tobias Eibach and Stefan Arnold, who went over parts of this thesis in its last stage and gave me valuable advice.

It is a pleasure to thank my supervisor Uwe Schöning for his stimulating suggestions and support during the research for this thesis, and I would also like to show my gratitude to Hans A. Kestler for his encouragement, support and motivating ideas. Without these two people, this work would not have been possible.

I want to thank my parents for their confidence in me and their never-ending support.

Especially, I want to express my deepest gratitude to Anja whose love encouraged me to complete this work.

Markus Maucher

Contents

1 Preliminaries 7
  1.1 Graphs 8
  1.2 Asymptotic behavior of functions 8
  1.3 Probability theory 11
  1.4 Computability and complexity 13

2 Different notions of (pseudo) randomness 17
  2.1 Notions of pseudorandomness 19
    2.1.1 Kolmogorov complexity and compressibility 19
    2.1.2 Statistical tests and Martin-Löf randomness 21
    2.1.3 Martingales and predictability 26
    2.1.4 Shannon Entropy 28
    2.1.5 Quasi-random sequences 30
  2.2 Pseudorandom Generators 32
  2.3 Influence on Algorithms 39

3 Algorithms and non-perfect randomness 43
  3.1 Testing the equality of polynomials 43
  3.2 Karger's algorithm for the minimum cut 48
  3.3 Schöning's random walk algorithm for the Boolean Satisfiability Problem 53

4 Randomized QuickSort 65
  4.1 An upper bound 70
  4.2 A lower bound 71
  4.3 Distributions with bounded entropy 73
  4.4 Randomness as a resource for the QuickSort algorithm 80

Contents

5 Local and population based search heuristics — **83**
- 5.1 Search Heuristics 84
  - 5.1.1 Simulated Annealing 84
  - 5.1.2 Population based heuristics 86
- 5.2 Implementation 90
- 5.3 Experimental Setup and Results 92
  - 5.3.1 Simulated Annealing 96
  - 5.3.2 Population based heuristics 111
  - 5.3.3 Discussion 125

6 Discussion of theoretical and experimental results — **127**

7 Major results of this thesis — **131**

8 Deutsche Zusammenfassung — **133**

Bibliography — **137**

Introduction

Throughout history, philosophers and scientists have tried to comprehend the concept of randomness. In his work "Physics" [2], Aristotle discusses "chance and spontaneity" as a possible cause of an observation that has to be considered when no other logical reasons can be found. But he also mentions other physicists who "found no place for chance among the causes which they recognized", while others "believe that chance is a cause, but that it is inscrutable to human intelligence, as being a divine thing and full of mystery." Many centuries later, in Newtonian mechanics, the world seemed to be (almost) completely explainable by physical laws, with randomness only being used where systems became too complex to be measured or calculated exactly. In other words, randomness was only considered a mathematical tool that could be used to model human insufficiencies. With the advent of quantum mechanics however, randomness became an important element of physics – Heisenberg's theory stated that some physical effects remained random ones, without the chance of exact measurements.

The notion of "quantitative randomness", i.e. the idea that the *amount* of randomness inherent to a random process should be expressed, has been thoroughly researched in the 20th century, e.g. by C.E. Shannon, A. N. Kolmogorov, R. Solomomoff and G. J. Chaitin. In 1948, C.E. Shannon published his work "A mathematical Theory of Communication" [3]. Initially addressing communication over noisy channels, his work was the foundation for a new branch of science, which is today known as information theory. Shannon introduced the notion of entropy for distributions on strings, making it possible to quantify the randomness of a discrete source of randomness. While this theory was initially intended to explain communication over an error-prone channel, it has also found its way into other areas like cryptography or even biology. Kolmogorov, Solomonoff and Chaitin followed a different approach: Instead of measuring the amount of randomness of a given probability distribution, they defined the

Contents

amount of randomness of individual bit strings – the Kolmogorov complexity of a string is defined as the shortest "program" that outputs that string. Chapter 2 of this thesis will give an introduction to these important notions.

In computer science, randomization is known as a valuable tool, with randomness being used in various ways, for example to avoid worst-case scenarios, or to find solutions that are hard to find in a deterministic way [4]. For example, when worst case and average case behavior differ, an input of an algorithm may be randomly altered to avoid the worst case. The randomized version of the sorting algorithm QuickSort [5], for example, determines randomly which elements to compare next. This way, it shows an expected complexity (measured in the number of comparisons) of order $n \log n$ when sorting *any* sequence of n numbers, while its deterministic version needs an order of n^2 comparisons for some worst case input sequences (cf. also [6]). For some problems, the best known deterministic versions are slower than the best known probabilistic ones. For example, the Miller-Rabin test, the fastest known algorithm to test if a given number is a prime is a randomized algorithm [7]. Until 2002 (published 2004), it wasn't even known if there exists a deterministic algorithm for that problem with polynomial complexity. That problem has been solved in [8], but the probabilistic algorithm is still widely in use because it is much faster than its deterministic counterpart.

If one doubts the random nature of an observed process, a statistical test can serve to expose that process as non-random: a statistic, i.e. a real-valued function of the observed variables, is calculated. Based on the assumption that the process is random (the so-called *null hypothesis*), the range of the statistic is divided into a set with large probability and one with very small probability. Common values for the probability of the last set are 5% or 1% or even smaller values. As long as the value of the statistic remains within the set of high probability, no conclusion about the randomness of the process is drawn. However, if the computed value lies in the set of very small probability, the process "does not pass the test" and thus is not considered random. Note however that a statistical test can only be used to strengthen the so-called "alternative hypothesis", i.e. to indicate that a process is *not* random. A single statistical test can never be used to confirm a positive statement of the form "Sequence s is random". (Actually, such a test does exist in theory, but it is not computable.) So when examining a sequence with the help of statistical tests, we can never be sure if the sequence is really of random origin, even if it passes all of our (finitely many) statistical tests.

While randomness is used in many algorithms, it is still a rather unnatural concept for a computer: The standard computer is a machine, a completely deterministic device. Any random, non-predictable behavior of a computer is usually considered a flaw – given a program and an input, the program should always compute the same output. If a programmer wants to involve randomness in a computation, that random information has to be collected from outside the system and treated like an additional input. Getting them from an external (physical) process is often expensive and relatively slow, so in most cases pseudo random numbers are used [9]. These numbers are initialized with one or a few random numbers, the so-called seed. Then from that seed a sequence of numbers is calculated that can be used instead of random numbers.

Astonishingly, most people are rather bad at spontaneously creating random sequences of bits or numbers [10]. Especially clusters of any type, like longer sequences of zeros in a binary sequence, are often considered non-random, and when people are requested to create a random sequence of bits, longer sequences are often avoided. Even everyday actions for creating random events with fair chances may be deceiving: When spinning a coin and watching if it falls heads or tails up, there can be a significant difference between the occurences of heads and tails [11].

When designing and analyzing randomized algorithms, one usually assumes a perfect source of randomness. In particular, the random numbers that are used are considered uniformly distributed and independent. Implementing randomized algorithms, however, one usually has to use pseudorandom numbers. Using such numbers may severely influence the quality of an algorithm's output. In Chapter 2 we will give two examples where the use of pseudorandom numbers has a strong influence on the success probability of randomized algorithms. In Section 3.1, we show that the repeated execution of a probabilistic algorithm may not reduce the total error probability to the desired degree if pseudorandom numbers are used. In Section 3.3, we show that a small bias in the distribution of the random source may have a strong influence on a random walk algorithm, in our case Schöning's random-walk algorithm for the 3-satisfiability problem.

Karloff et al. [12] and Bach [13] showed that some algorithms, like QuickSort or primality testing, have bad running times or even yield wrong results when used with unsuitable pseudo-random number generators. Karloff et al. also showed that a good average case behavior can be guaranteed by the right kind of pseudorandom generator. In the case of QuickSort, they proved a good average case behavior of order $n \log n$ when using an explicit polynomial generator (see Section 2.2), while the use of a linear congruential generator can lead to running times of order n^2. List gave an upper bound for the running time of QuickSort that depends on the probability distribution of the pivot element (cf. [14]). In Section 4.2, we complement this result with a lower bound and show how the min-entropy of a random source determines the number of comparisons needed by QuickSort. In Section 4.4, we show that the number of random bits consumed by the QuickSort algorithm can increase from n to $n \log n$ when non-perfect random numbers are used, although the number of random choices does not depend on the quality of the random numbers.

Search heuristics for combinatorial problems like the Traveling Salesman Problem or the Boolean Satisfiability Problem often involve random choices in their search. Several properties of random search can lead to advantages over deterministic approaches. For example, random choices may help to lead away from local optima without the need for storing too much information, a property that the Simulated Annealing heuristic benefits greatly from. Random choices also help to avoid worst case inputs. Apart from that, random choices allow the user to run a search algorithm several times, even in parallel, increasing the probability of finding a good solution. In this thesis, we investigated how the choice of the random generator influences the solution of a search heuristics. Meysenburg for example showed experimentally that a simple genetic algorithm led to comparable results, independent from the choice of the random number generator (see [15, 16]). Tompkins and Hoos showed experimentally that stochastic local search methods for the satisfiability problem are not influenced by the quality of the pseudorandom number generator [17]. However, both of these works considered the use of standard random number generators. In contrast, we were rather interested in the effects of generators with very low quality. To this end, we artificially reduced the quality of random sources and experimentally measured the effect on Simulated Annealing and Genetic Algorithms. The main characteristics of the random source we altered were its bias, dependence and period length. We also used quasi-random sequences in order to see if randomness was needed at all. To this end, we conducted several experiments where we gradually decreased the quality of our pseudorandom number generator and tested if this decrease in quality directly affected the output of our search heuristics. The results for Simulated Annealing are presented in Section 5.3.1 and the results for the genetic algorithm are presented in Section 5.3.2.

Contents

1 Preliminaries

In this thesis, $\mathbb{N}$ will denote the set of natural numbers, $\mathbb{R}$ the set of real numbers, $\mathbb{R}^{\geq 0}$ the set of non-negative real numbers, $\mathbb{Q}$ the set of rational numbers and $\mathbb{Q}^{\geq 0}$ the set of non-negative rational numbers.

For any finite set Σ, let Σ^* be the set of all finite sequences of elements from Σ. E.g. $\{0,1\}^*$ denotes the set of all finite bit sequences. By Σ^∞ we denote the set of all infinite sequences over Σ. The empty sequence is denoted by $\bot$.

When convenient, sequences will be given in string notation, without parentheses and delimiters. E.g., the sequence $(0,1,1,0,1,1,0)$ is then written as a bit string 0110110.

For a finite sequence $x = x_0 x_1 \ldots x_{n-1}$, $l(x)$ denotes the *length* of x, for example $l(0110110) = 7$.

Given a finite sequence $x = x_1 x_2 \ldots x_n$ resp. an infinite sequence $y = y_1 y_2 y_3 \ldots$. Then the sequence $\tilde{x} = x_1 x_2 \ldots x_k$ is called a prefix of x and $\hat{x} = x_k x_{k+1} \ldots x_n$ is called a suffix of x, for $1 \leq k \leq n$. Analogously, $\tilde{y} = y_1 y_2 y_k \ldots$ is a prefix of y and $\hat{y} = y_k y_{k+1} y_{k+2} \ldots$ is a suffix of y. Formally, $\bot$ is prefix and suffix of any sequence, and any sequence is prefix and suffix of itself.

For any set A, 2^A will describe the power set of A, i.e. the set of all subsets of A.

A *multiset* is a generalization of a set that can contain elements multiple times. The multiplicity of an element x in a multiset S is the number of times x is contained in S. For example, the multiset $S = \{a, b, b, b, c, c\}$ contains 6 elements. The multiplicity of a in S is 1, that of b is 3, and that of c is 2. A multiset S_1 is a subset of a multiset S_2 if for all $x \in S_1$, the multiplicity of x in S_1 is not larger than the multiplicity of x in S_2. We then write $S_1 \subseteq S_2$.

1 Preliminaries

1.1 Graphs

A *graph* $G = (V,E)$ consists of a set of vertices $V = \{v_1,\ldots,v_n\}$ and a set of edges $E \subseteq 2^V$ with $|e| = 2$ for all $e \in E$. A *multigraph* $G = (V,E)$ is a graph where E is a multiset of edges, i.e. two vertices can be connected by multiple edges.

A path in a graph $G = (V,E)$ from $u \in V$ to $v \in V$ is a finite sequence of vertices $u = v_{i_1}, v_{i_2}, \ldots, v_{i_{k-1}}, v_{i_k} = v$ such that $\{v_{i_j}, v_{i_{j+1}}\} \in E$ for all $1 \leq j \leq k-1$. The graph is *connected* if there is a path from u to v for all vertices $u, v \in V$.

1.2 Asymptotic behavior of functions

Considering the running time or error probability of algorithms, we are often mainly interested in the dominating term of a function rather than the exact function. Here Landau notation is useful to describe the asymptotic behavior of a function.

Definition 1 *Given a function* $f : \mathbb{N} \to \mathbb{R}^{\geq 0}$, *define the sets*

- $O(f(n)) = \{g : \mathbb{N} \to \mathbb{R}^{\geq 0} \mid \exists c, n_0 > 0 : \forall n \geq n_0 : g(n) \leq cf(n)\}$,
- $\Omega(f(n)) = \{g : \mathbb{N} \to \mathbb{R}^{\geq 0} \mid \exists c, n_0 > 0 : \forall n \geq n_0 : g(n) \geq cf(n)\}$,
- $\Theta(f(n)) = O(f(n)) \cap \Omega(f(n))$,
- $o(f(n)) = \{g : \mathbb{N} \to \mathbb{R}^{\geq 0} \mid \forall c > 0 : \exists n_0 > 0 : \forall n \geq n_0 : g(n) \leq cf(n)\}$,
- $\omega(f(n)) = \{g : \mathbb{N} \to \mathbb{R}^{\geq 0} \mid \forall c > 0 : \exists n_0 > 0 : \forall n \geq n_0 : g(n) \geq cf(n)\}$.

Instead of $f(n) \in O(g(n))$ *we also use the common notation* $f(n) = O(g(n))$; *analogously for the other notations. We also define*

- $\tilde{O}(f(n)) = \{g : \mathbb{N} \to \mathbb{R}^{\geq 0} \mid \exists n_0 > 0, \text{ polynomial } p : \forall n \geq n_0 : g(n) \leq p(n)f(n)\}$,

and write $f(n) \asymp g(n)$ *if* $f(n) \in \tilde{O}(g(n))$ *and* $g(n) \in \tilde{O}(f(n))$.

The Master Theorem presents a valuable tool in solving a common type of recursions, for example for the analysis of divide-and-conquer algorithms:

1.2 Asymptotic behavior of functions

Theorem 1.1 (Master Theorem) *Let T be recursion of the form*

$$T(n) = aT\left(\frac{n}{b}\right) + \Theta(n^k)$$

with $a, b \geq 1$ and $k \geq 1$. then the recursion can be bounded as follows:

$$T(n) = \begin{cases} \Theta(n^k) & \text{if } a < b^k \\ \Theta(n^k \log n) & \text{if } a = b^k \\ \Theta(n^{\log b / \log a}) & \text{if } a > b^k \end{cases}$$

For a proof of this theorem, see for example [18].

In Chapter 3 we will need the following lemma.

Lemma 1.1 *For any fixed $x \in \mathbb{Q}^{\geq 0}$,*

$$\prod_{i=1}^{n} \frac{i}{i+x} = \Theta\left(\frac{1}{n^x}\right).$$

Proof. For $x \in \mathbb{N}$,

$$\prod_{i=1}^{n} \frac{i}{i+x} = \frac{1 \cdot 2 \cdots (n-1) \cdot n}{(1+x)(2+x) \cdots (n-1+x)(n+x)} = \frac{1 \cdot 2 \cdots x}{(n+1) \cdots (n+x)} = \Theta\left(\frac{1}{n^x}\right).$$

Now let $x := \frac{a}{b}$ for $a, b \in \mathbb{N}$. Then we have

$$\left(\prod_{i=1}^{n} \frac{i}{i+x}\right)^b = \left(\prod_{i=1}^{n} \frac{ib}{ib+a}\right)^b \leq \prod_{j=0}^{b-1} \prod_{i=1}^{n} \frac{ib+j}{ib+a+j} = \prod_{i=b}^{(n-1)b-1} \frac{i}{i+a}$$

$$= \frac{b \cdot (b+1) \cdots (b+a-1)}{(n-1)b((n-1)b+1) \cdots ((n-1)b-1+a)} = O\left(\frac{1}{n^a}\right),$$

using the fact that $\frac{x}{y} < \frac{x+a}{y+a}$ for $0 < x < y$ and $a > 0$. In the same way we can show

$$\left(\prod_{i=1}^{n} \frac{i}{i+x}\right)^b = \left(\prod_{i=1}^{n} \frac{ib}{ib+a}\right)^b \geq \prod_{j=1}^{b} \prod_{i=1}^{n} \frac{(i-1)b+j}{(i-1)b+a+j} = \prod_{i=1}^{nb} \frac{i}{i+a}$$

$$= \frac{1 \cdot 2 \cdots a}{(nb+1)(nb+2) \cdots (nb+a)} = \Omega\left(\frac{1}{n^a}\right).$$

1 Preliminaries

Combining the two inequalities finishes our proof. ∎

Note: For k not too small, we can also give the estimation

$$\prod_{i=k}^{n} \frac{i}{i+x} \approx \left(\frac{k}{n}\right)^x.$$

This can be derived as follows. For $x \in \mathbb{N}$, we have

$$\prod_{i=k}^{n} \frac{i}{i+x} = \frac{k(k+1)\cdots(k+x-1)}{(n+1)(n+2)\cdots(n+x)} \approx \left(\frac{k}{n}\right)^x.$$

For $x = a/b$, we get

$$\begin{aligned}\left(\prod_{i=k}^{n} \frac{i}{i+x}\right)^b &= \left(\prod_{i=k}^{n} \frac{ib}{ib+a}\right)^b \leq \prod_{j=0}^{b-1}\prod_{i=k}^{n} \frac{ib+j}{ib+a+j} \\ &= \frac{kb\cdot(kb+1)\cdots(kb+a-1)}{(n+1)b\cdot((n+1)b+1)\cdots((n+1)b+a-1)} \\ &\leq \left(\frac{kb+a}{nb+b}\right)^a \approx \left(\frac{k}{n}\right)^a,\end{aligned}$$

and similarly

$$\begin{aligned}\left(\prod_{i=k}^{n} \frac{i}{i+x}\right)^b &= \left(\prod_{i=k}^{n} \frac{ib}{ib+a}\right)^b \geq \prod_{j=1}^{b}\prod_{i=k}^{n} \frac{(i-1)b+j}{(i-1)b+a+j} \\ &= \frac{((k-1)b+1)\cdot((k-1)b+2)\cdots((k-1)b+a)}{(nb+1)\cdot(nb+2)\cdots(nb+a)} \\ &\geq \left(\frac{kb-b}{nb+a}\right)^a \approx \left(\frac{k}{n}\right)^a.\end{aligned}$$

These two inequalities can then be combined to

$$\prod_{i=k}^{n} \frac{i}{i+\frac{a}{b}} \approx \left(\frac{k}{n}\right)^{\frac{a}{b}}.$$

1.3 Probability theory

Definition 2 *A* **probability space** *is a triple* $(\Omega, \mathcal{F}, P)$, *where* Ω *is a set (called the* **sample space***),* $\mathcal{F} \subseteq 2^{\Omega}$ *is a* σ*-algebra (the set of* **events***), and P is a measure (the* **probability measure***, or* **distribution***) on* $(\Omega, \mathcal{F})$ *with* $P(\Omega) = 1$.

In this thesis, we only consider discrete probability spaces, i.e. Ω will always be countable. In that case, we can define $\mathcal{F} := 2^{\Omega}$, introduce a function $p : \Omega \to [0,1]$ with $\sum_{\omega \in \Omega} p(\omega) = 1$ and define $P(A) := \sum_{\omega \in A} p(\omega)$ for any event $A \in \mathcal{F}$.

For any event B with $P(B) > 0$, the **conditional probability** $P(A \mid B)$ *("the probability of A given B")* is defined as $P(A \mid B) := \frac{P(A \cap B)}{P(B)}$.

A function $X : \Omega \to \mathbb{R}$ is called a **random variable**. We will write $P(X \in B)$ as an abbreviation for $P(\{\omega \mid X(\omega) \in B\})$ resp. $P(X = x)$ for $P(\{\omega \mid X(\omega) = x\})$. X is a **discrete** random variable if X only takes a countable number of different values, i.e. $X(\Omega) := \{X(\omega) \mid \omega \in \Omega\}$ is countable.

For two probability spaces $(\Omega, \mathcal{F}, P_1)$ and $(\Omega, \mathcal{F}, P_2)$, we can assign random variables to these probability spaces: The notations $X \sim P_1$ resp. $Y \sim P_2$ define the abbreviation $P(X = x) := P_1(X = x)$ resp. $P(Y = y) := P_2(Y = y)$.

The **expected value** $E(X)$ of a random variable X is $E(X) := \sum_{\omega \in \Omega} P(\omega) X(\omega)$. This is equivalent to $E(X) = \sum_{x \in X(\Omega)} x \cdot P(X = x)$. The **variance** $V(X)$ of a random variable X is defined as $V(x) := E((X - E(X))^2)$.

A sequence of random variables $X_1, X_2, \ldots$ is **k-wise independent** if any subsequence $X_{i_1}, \ldots, X_{i_k}$ of length k is independent, i.e. for any $x_1, \ldots, x_k$ and $i_1, \ldots, i_k \in \mathbb{N}$

$$P(X_{i_1} = x_1, \ldots, X_{i_k} = x_k) = \prod_{j=1}^{k} P(X_{i_j} = x_j) \ .$$

For $k = 2$ we call such a sequence **pairwise independent**. If a sequence is k-wise independent for all $k \in \mathbb{N}$, we call it **independent**.

A discrete random variable X is **uniformly distributed** if $P(X = i) = P(X = j)$ for all $i, j \in X(\Omega)$.

1 Preliminaries

Definition 3 *An infinite sequence of random variables $X_0, X_1, X_2, \ldots$ is called Markov chain if it has the property*

$$\forall k > 0 : P(X_{k+1} = x \mid X_0 = x_0, \ldots, X_k = x_k) = P(X_{k+1} = x \mid X_k = x_k) \ ,$$

i.e. the value of X_{k+1} only depends on the value of X_k. The Markov chain is called time-homogenous if it has the additional property

$$\forall k > 0 : P(X_{k+1} = x \mid X_k = y) = P(X_k = x \mid X_{k-1} = y) \ .$$

The following lemma will be used in Chapter 4 to bound the binary entropy function by a polynomial term:

Lemma 1.2 *Let H be the binary entropy function, i.e.*

$$H(x) = -x\log_2(x) - (1-x)\log_2(1-x) \ .$$

Then for all integers $n \geq 1$ and i with $0 \leq i \leq n$,

$$\frac{(i-1)^2}{n^2} + \frac{(n-i)^2}{n^2} + H\left(\frac{i}{n+1}\right) \geq 1.$$

Proof. We use the inequalities $-\ln(1-x) \geq x$ resp. $-\log_2(1-x) \geq \frac{x}{\ln 2}$, that hold for $0 \leq x \leq 1$. For $n \geq 5$ this leads to

$$\frac{(i-1)^2}{n^2} + \frac{(n-i)^2}{n^2} + H\left(\frac{i}{n+1}\right)$$

$$= \frac{i^2 - 2i + 1 + n^2 - 2in + i^2}{n^2}$$

$$\quad - \frac{i}{n+1}\log_2\frac{i}{n+1} - \left(1 - \frac{i}{n+1}\right)\log_2\left(1 - \frac{i}{n+1}\right)$$

$$= \frac{2i^2 - 2i + 1 + n^2 - 2in}{n^2}$$

$$\quad - \frac{i}{n+1}\log_2\left(1 - \frac{n-i+1}{n+1}\right) - \frac{n-i+1}{n+1}\log_2\left(1 - \frac{i}{n+1}\right)$$

$$\geq \frac{2i^2 - 2i + 1 + n^2 - 2in}{n^2} + \left(\frac{i}{n+1} \cdot \frac{n-i+1}{n+1} + \frac{n-i+1}{n+1} \cdot \frac{i}{n+1}\right) / \ln 2$$

$$\geq \frac{2i^2 - 2i + 1 + n^2 - 2in + 2in - 2i^2 + 2i}{n^2} = \frac{n^2 + 1}{n^2} \geq 1$$

For the second to last inequality, we use the fact that $(n+1)^2 \ln 2 \leq n^2$ for all $n \geq 5$. The remaining 14 cases $(n,i) = (1,0), (1,1), \ldots, (4,4)$ can be checked by computer. ∎

1.4 Computability and complexity

When talking about computability and complexity, a standard model of computation is needed – a model of a simple but powerful computing device. It should be simple enough to allow elegant proofs about what it can or can't do; and it should be powerful enough so that it can compute the same functions that a modern computer can compute. The Turing machine is the standard model of computation that unites these properties.

Definition 4 *A Turing machine M is a simplified model of a computer. It consists of several (finitely many) states, where one of these states is the initial state and one or more states are final states. The memory is represented by these states and a one-dimensional tape that is infinitely large in both directions. Each position of the tape may contain an element of the* work alphabet Γ, *which contains a special symbol $\square$, called "blank". The internal state of the Turing machine can be described by the actual state, the position on the tape, and the content of the tape. At the start of a computation, the Turing machine is in the inital state, the tape contains only the input, expressed in the* input alphabet $\Sigma \subseteq \Gamma - \{\square\}$, *with all other positions on the tape equal to $\square$, and the position of the machine is at the leftmost symbol of the input. The behavior of a Turing machine during a computation is determined by its transition rule. For each state and symbol at the actual tape position, the transition rule specifies the new symbol at that position, the new state and the new position at the next time step. The new position may differ from the last one by -1, 0 or 1, i.e. the machine can move one position to the left or right, or stay at its current position. The computation ends when the machine reaches a final state. The result of the computation is defined as the content of the tape after the computation, excluding $\square$ symbols. If the tape only consists of $\square$ symbols, the result is the empty string $\perp$. If the machine does not stop in a final state (i.e. runs in an infinite loop of non-final states), the result is* undefined.

We say that a Turing machine M computes a function $f : \{0,1\}^* \to \{0,1\}^*$, if for every input $x \in \{0,1\}^*$, M computes $f(x)$. M computes a function $f : \mathbb{N} \to \mathbb{N}$, if for

1 Preliminaries

every $x \in \mathbb{N}$, M computes the binary representation of $f(x)$ if its input is a binary representation of x. Computations of functions $f : \mathbb{N} \to \{0,1\}^*$ and $f : \{0,1\}^* \to \mathbb{N}$ are defined analogously.

We say that a Turing machine M *accepts* a language $L \subseteq \{0,1\}^*$, if M computes L's characteristic function c_L with

$$c_L(x) := \begin{cases} 0 & \text{if } x \notin L \\ 1 & \text{if } x \in L \end{cases}$$

Now that we have defined our model of computation, we can talk about computability:

Definition 5 *A function $f : \{0,1\}^* \to \{0,1\}^*$ is* computable *(or* recursive*), if there is a Turing machine M that computes f. We say a set $S \subseteq \{0,1\}^*$ is* computable *(or* recursive*), if its characteristic function c_S is computable.*

A set $S \subseteq \{0,1\}^*$ is recursively enumerable *if S is the range of a total computable function $f : \{0,1\}^* \to \{0,1\}^*$, i.e. $S = \{f(1), f(2), f(3), \ldots\}$.*

A function $f : \mathbb{N} \to \mathbb{N}$ is recursively enumerable*, if its graph G_f is recursively enumerable, with $G_f := \{(x,y) \mid y \leq f(x)\}$.*

Since any infinite bit sequence $x \in \{0,1\}^*$ can be interpreted as a function $f : \mathbb{N} \to \{0,1\}$ or set $S \subseteq \mathbb{N}$, the definition of recursive enumerability can be applied to sequences.

Even if we know that a function or set is computable, we might want to be more precise about the difficulty of computing this set or function. To this end, we need the definitions of some standard complexity classes.

Definition 6 *For any Turing machine M, define $\text{time}_M(x)$ as the number of steps of M with input x until M reaches a terminal state.*

A language $L \subseteq \{0,1\}^*$ lies in the complexity class P if L is accepted by some Turing machine M and there exists a polynomial p such that for every string $x \in \{0,1\}^*$,

1.4 Computability and complexity

$\text{time}_M(x) \leq p(|x|)$. I.e. M's running time increases only polynomially in the length of the input x.

A language $L \subseteq \{0,1\}^*$ is in BPP if a Turing machine M and two polynomials p and q exist with the following properties:

1. For every $x \in \{0,1\}^*$ and every $y \in \{0,1\}^{q(x)}$, $\text{time}_M(x,y) \leq p(|x|)$
2. If $Y \in \{0,1\}^{q(x)}$ is a uniformly distributed random variable,

$$P[M(x,Y) = c_L(x)] \geq \frac{2}{3} \text{ for every } x \in \{0,1\}^* ,$$

i.e. M computes the characteristic function of L, and gives a correct answer with probability at least $2/3$.

A language $L \subseteq \{0,1\}^*$ lies in the complexity class NP if there is a Turing machine M and a polynomial p with the following properties:

1. For every $x, y \in \{0,1\}^*$, $\text{time}_M(x,y) \leq p(|x|)$,
2. For every $x \notin L$ and $y \in \{0,1\}^*$, $M(x,y) = 0$,
3. For every $x \in L$ there exists $y \in \{0,1\}^*$ with $M(x,y) = 1$.

A language $L \subseteq \{0,1\}^*$ lies in the complexity class P/poly if there is a Turing machine M and two polynomials p and q with the following properties:

1. For every $x, y \in \{0,1\}^*$, $\text{time}_M(x,y) \leq p(|x|)$,
2. For every $n \in \mathbb{N}$ there exists a $y_n \in \{0,1\}^{q(n)}$ such that for every $x \in \{0,1\}^n$ $M(x,y_n) = c_L(x)$.

Essentially, the languages in all complexity classes in Definition 6 are accepted by some Turing machine M in polynomial time. However, M always (except for the class P) may depend on a so called "advice string" y: For L to be in BPP, a large part of all candidates for y must lead to the correct result; for $P/poly$, there is only one advice string for every *length* of the input; for NP, the existence of one advice string per input is sufficient.

1 Preliminaries

2 Different notions of (pseudo) randomness

Random numbers play a vital role in many areas of computer science. In cryptography, for example, pairs of public and private keys are chosen at random. In simulation, only statistical facts about a physical phenomenon may be known. In optimization, choices are frequently made at random when the optimal choice cannot be calculated effectively. And often, probabilistic algorithms are faster than any known deterministic algorithm for the same problem. But random numbers are not an integral part of a computer system. Since computers are purely deterministic systems, random behavior only occurs in the case of a system error. The only way to obtain "real random numbers" in a computer is by using random input from outside the system. Options include using the system time, measuring times between a user's keystrokes, or measuring other physical effects that are supposed to be random. Since input is usually processed much slower than internal data and, depending on the source of randomness, random numbers may only be available at a slow rate, a common approach uses these random numbers as a so-called *seed* for a longer sequence of pseudorandom numbers: From this seed, a much longer sequence is calculated in a deterministic way, assuming that this new sequence leads to a similar result as a sequence of real random numbers of the same length would. One of the first methods of this kind was the linear congruential generator, short lcg. This generator starts with a random number x (the seed) and successively applies a linear function $f(x) = ax + b \mod m$ to the last value, generating a sequence $(x, f(x), f^2(x), f^3(x), \ldots)$, assuming that this sequence can be used instead of a sequence of random numbers.

Randomness is used with different goals in mind: In cryptography, the main goal is to provide numbers that cannot be guessed by an attacker; in simulation,

2 Different notions of (pseudo) randomness

using the random numbers provided by the computer should lead to the same result as in a real world process; in optimization, expected running times or results should be similar to those when using random numbers. Pseudorandom numbers have another property that is valuable in some cases: By saving the seed, we can efficiently save the whole pseudorandom sequence. This allows to reproduce simulation results, or to synchronize cryptographic processes that need to share sequences of random numbers.

In this chapter, we will sum up various methods to define randomness and describe the advantages and disadvantages of these notions as well as equivalences between them. We give some examples where pseudorandom numbers are used, how such numbers can be produced and where their quality affects the outcome of algorithms.

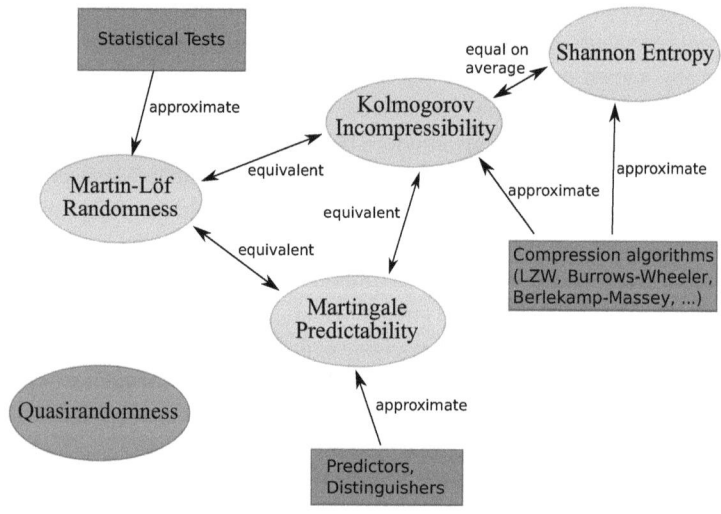

Figure 2.1: Various notions of pseudorandomness

In Section 2.1, we will sum up Kolmogorov's notion of incompressibility and Martin-Löf's definition of algorithmic randomness, explain the basics of martingale theory and predictability, and give some insight into Shannon's information theoretic entropy. Additionally, the notion of quasi-randomness will be explained. In Section 2.2, we will list the most commonly used pseudorandom number generators, those used in practice as well as those found in some theoretical results. In section 2.3, we will give an overview of connections between the quality of pseudorandom generators and their influence on algorithms.

2.1 Notions of pseudorandomness

In this section, we introduce various methods to measure the "randomness" in a sequence of bits or numbers. After some mathematical preliminaries, we will begin with the notion of Kolmogorov complexity. We will then move on to statistical tests and Per Martin-Löf's definition of algorithmic randomness, describe the theory of martingales and their connection to predictability and distinguishability and explain C.E. Shannon's notion of information-theoretic entropy.

2.1.1 Kolmogorov complexity and compressibility

Kolmogorov complexity was independently introduced by Solomonoff, Kolmogorov and Chaitin. It measures with how many bits an object, usually a binary string, can be described, where every object has to be described in a given "language". A core principle of Kolmogorov complexity is the notion of non-compressibility: If we want to find a short description for a bit string of length n, saving at least l bits, we only have a very limited choice: There are only 2^{n+1-l} strings of length up to $n-l$, so we can compress at most a fraction of 2^{-l+1} of our strings. The rest can't be compressed by those l bits. Kolmogorov complexity uses this fact to disqualify strings as non-random: The probability that a random string can be compressed by l bits is about 2^{-l}. So, if a string can be compressed much, it is probably not random.

Definition 7 *Let $M_1, M_2, M_3, \ldots$ be a recursive enumeration of all Turing machines. By $M_i(x)$ we denote the output of M_i when it's run with input x. A* **universal Turing machine** *is a Turing machine M_u with*

$$M_u(i, x) = M_i(x) \ .$$

2 Different notions of (pseudo) randomness

The Kolmogorov complexity $C(x)$ of a string x is defined as

$$C(x) := \min\{l(i) \mid M_i(\varepsilon) = x\} \ .$$

An infinite sequence $s \in \{0,1\}^\infty$ is Kolmogorov-random, if for every prefix $s_{1..n}$ of s the condition $C(s_{1..n}) \geq n - c$ holds for a constant c.

According to this definition, the Turing machine M_u acts as an interpreter of other Turing machines: It is able to simulate any other Turing machine with any input. That way, every binary string x can be described by describing a Turing machine that outputs x.

In the definition of Kolmogorov complexity, no concrete universal Turing machine is given, so that we could use different universal Turing machines in the definition. Actually, using a different Turing machine wouldn't be a big change. The *Invariance Theorem* states that using different universal Turing machines only results in a constant difference between the Kolmogorov complexities of any string x, where this constants only depends on the two universal Turing machines, but not on x.

A major disadvantage of Kolmogorov complexity is its non-computability. So it is not possible to exactly compute $C(x)$ for all strings x. It is, however, possible to give an approximation of $C(x)$. Looking for the shortest description d of a string x is equivalent to compressing x, where d can then be decompressed by the universal machine M_u. We can approximate this compression with standard compression algorithms, like `zip` or `bzip2`. For a fixed compression algorithm Z we can then define a string to be (Z,k)-random if Z cannot compress the string by more than k bits.

An interesting approach to describe a sequence of numbers is to assume that the sequence was generated by a linear recursion of some degree k, i.e. for all $i > k$,

$$X_i = a_0 + \sum_{j=1}^{k} a_j X_{i-j}$$

for some coefficients $a_0, \ldots, a_k$. In the case of a binary sequence, all these numbers are 0 or 1 and the recursion corresponds to a linear feedback shift register. A sequence can then be described by $X_1, \ldots, X_k$ and $a_0, \ldots, a_k$. For any given

2.1 Notions of pseudorandomness

sequence, the linear degree k of that sequence can be efficiently found by the Berlekamp-Massey algorithm [19].

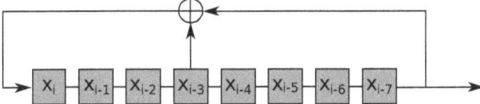

Figure 2.2: A linear feedback shift register with the recursion $X_i = X_{i-3} + X_{i-7}$

Definition 8 *For a finite sequence $x = (x_1, \ldots, x_n)$ the linear complexity of x, short $\mathrm{lc}(x)$, is the smallest k such that for all $i > k$,*

$$x_i = a_0 + \sum_{j=1}^{k} a_j x_{i-j}$$

for some parameters $a_0, a_1, \ldots, a_k$.

For an infinite sequence x, its linear complexity is a function lc_x with

$$\mathrm{lc}_x(i) = \mathrm{lc}(x_1, \ldots, x_i) \ .$$

For example, the linear complexity of a linear congruential generator is 1. It is easy to see that the linear complexity of every sequence $x \in \{0, \ldots, m-1\}^{2k}$ is at most k: For every $i > k$, suppose x_i is determined by the equation $x_i = a_0 + \sum_{j=1}^{k} a_j x_{i-j}$. Then we can find $a_0, a_1, \ldots, a_k$ by solving the system of all these equations for $x_{k+1}, \ldots, x_{2k}$.

2.1.2 Statistical tests and Martin-Löf randomness

In statistics, when sampling from a distribution D, a common method to test if a sample X was really drawn from distribution D is to divide the sample space S into two sets: the set S_1 of "typical" outcomes and the set S_0 of "non-typical" outcomes such that $P(X \in S_0) = \varepsilon$ for some small ε. If $X \in S_0$, that variable could still be sampled according to D, but there is at least a reason to be suspicious.

2 Different notions of (pseudo) randomness

Definition 9 *Let S be a sample space, D be a probability distribution on S and X a random variable with $X \sim D$.*

A function $f : S \to \{0,1\}$ with $P[f(X) = 1] = 1 - \varepsilon$ is called a **statistical test** *for D with confidence level ε. We say a sample x passes the test f (or f accepts x) if $f(x) = 1$. Otherwise x doesn't pass f (or f rejects x).*

For example, consider a uniform distribution on the set $S = \{0,1\}^{32}$ of all 32-bit strings. We could just look at the first 10 bits of a random string X and reject X if each of these 10 bits is a zero. Only a fraction of 2^{-10} of all strings in S start with 10 zeros, so we would reject a true random sample with a probability lower than 0.1%. This confidence level could be easily changed by choosing one or more different prefixes.

Note that in the definition above, f computes the characteristic function of S_1. It is not clear which elements of S should belong to S_0: from a statistical point of view, all sets S_0 with $P[X \in S_0] = \varepsilon$ are equally well suited. In practice, S_1 often consists of those sequences that have desirable properties, like equidistribution or pairwise independence, or simply properties that are easy and fast to compute. Ideally, a good pseudorandom sequence would pass all statistical tests, at least with probability of about $1 - \varepsilon$. However, pseudorandom generators are usually designed to output exponentially many numbers from a small seed, say 2^n numbers from a seed of length n. So when outputting a sequence of length l, only one out of 2^n sequences can be output, while a true random process would output one out of all possible 2^l sequences. By putting all those 2^n sequences into S_0, we can construct a statistical test where ε decreases exponentially when the sequence length l is increased. So technically, for every pseudorandom generator g and every confidence level ε, there is a statistical test with that confidence level that rejects the output of g. It is not clear, however, if this can be done by an efficient test. To be practically usable, a statistical test's running time should be a polynomial in $1/\varepsilon$.

The following properties are commonly tested by statistical tests:

Frequencies of patterns The simplest of these tests just count the number of zeros or ones in a sequence. These should not differ too much. More sophisticated tests count frequencies of certain patterns, either overlapping ones or non-overlapping ones. Instead of counting the frequencies of all patterns up to a certain length, one can also restrict oneself to patterns of special forms. Examples for this kind of test are the run test, which counts the length of runs of zeros or ones (either in the whole sequence or in each k-bit block) or the poker test, which divides the set of all patterns into classes known from the poker card game (like one pair, two pairs, full house, etc.).

Compressibility This kind of test tries to compress a given sequence. A truly random sequence usually isn't compressible (see Section 2.1.1). Compression can be measured by methods like the Lempel-Ziv algorithm, the Burrows-Wheeler transform or the Berlekamp-Massey algorithm. A further approach can be made via non-lossless compression: A cosinus or fourier transform can show if a sequence can be approximated by few base vectors of a given transform.

Random walks Tests from this class use the bits of a sequence to run a simple randomized algorithm. The random excursion test, for example, simulates a random walk on a line, walking in one direction each time a "0" comes up, and walking in the other direction for every "1". This random walk shouldn't wander too far away from the starting point, but it shouldn't stay too close to it for the whole run, either. This test is generalized in the cumulative sum test, that interprets bit blocks as integers and examines their cumulative sums.

More There exist many more tests. Actually any property of a sequence can be used to design a statistical test, as long as that property can be measured and something about its stochastic behavior when observed on a random sequence is known. Depending on the distribution of such a property, there are various tests that may be appropriate, like the χ^2 test for testing the variance of a value under a normal distribution.

For further insight into statistical tests, see [9]. Statistical tests cannot only be used to qualify random processes as random or non-random, they can also be used to compare if two random processes incorporate different probability distributions. We will briefly describe two statistical tests of this class that can be used to find out if the outputs of two algorithms are statistically different.

2 Different notions of (pseudo) randomness

- Welch's t test: Given a group of observations $x_1,\ldots,x_n \in \mathbb{R}$ and another group $y_1,\ldots,y_m \in \mathbb{R}$, Welch's t statistics is defined as

$$t = \frac{\overline{X}-\overline{Y}}{\sqrt{\frac{s_X^2}{n}+\frac{s_Y^2}{m}}},$$

where $\overline{X}$ and $\overline{Y}$ are the sample means of the two groups and s_X^2 and s_Y^2 are unbiased estimators of the sample variations of the two groups. This statistic approximately follows a Student's t distribution. It can be used to test if the mean of one distribution is greater than the mean of the other distribution (and thus also if their means are different).

- Mann-Whitney U test: Given two groups of observations of equal size $x_1,\ldots,x_n \in \mathbb{R}$ and $y_1,\ldots,y_m \in \mathbb{R}$, let r_i be the *rank* of x_i in the union of the two sets $\{x_1,\ldots,x_n,y_1,\ldots,y_n\}$ for $1 \leq i \leq n$. Then the *Mann-Whitney U statistics* is defined as

$$\sum_{i=1}^{n} r_i - \frac{n(n+1)}{2}.$$

This test statistic is approximately Gaussian distributed. It can be used to test if one distribution is "statistically greater" than another distribution in the sense that $P(X > Y) > 0.5$ where X is drawn from one distribution and Y from the other.

A more formal approach concerning statistical tests and randomness has been made by P. Martin-Löf in 1966 [20]. He formally defined algorithmically random sequences of infinite length.

Definition 10 *A recursively enumerable set $T \subseteq \mathbb{N} \times \{0,1\}^*$ is a* **Martin-Löf test** *if, with $T_n := \{t \in \{0,1\}^* \mid (n,t) \in T\}$,*

$$\sum_{t \in T_n} 2^{-|t|} \leq 2^{-n}.$$

A sequence s in $\{0,1\}^\infty$ passes the test T if

$$s \notin \bigcap_n \bigcup_{t \in T_n} \{u \in \{0,1\}^\infty \mid t \text{ is a prefix of } u\}\ .$$

A sequence s is Martin-Löf random, if it passes all Martin-Löf tests.

2.1 Notions of pseudorandomness

For any $n \in \mathbb{N}$, the set T_n specifies a set of prefixes such that a random string in $\{0,1\}^*$ begins with a prefix from T_n with probability at most 2^{-n}. For example, consider the test $T = \{(n, 0^{n+1}), (n, 1^{n+1}) \mid n \geq 1\}$. Then $T_n = \{0^{n+1}, 1^{n+1}\}$, i.e. at "confidence level" n, the test would reject any string where the first $n+1$ bits are all zero or all one. According to the definition, this test would only reject the infinite string that entirely consists of ones and the one that entirely consists of zeros.

If s is a sequence drawn randomly under the uniform distribution from $\{0,1\}^\infty$ then for any fixed $t \in \{0,1\}^*$, t is a prefix of s with probability $2^{-|t|}$. Therefore, for any n, the set $\cup_{t \in T_n} \{u \in \{0,1\}^\infty \mid t \text{ is a prefix of } u\}$ is a set of measure at most 2^{-n}. Thus, the set $\cap_n \cup_{t \in T_n} \{u \in \{0,1\}^\infty \mid t \text{ is a prefix of } u\}$ is a set of measure 0. Since there are only countably many Martin-Löf tests, and the union of countably many sets of measure 0 has itself measure 0, the set of sequences that are not Martin-Löf random has measure 0. This means that the set of Martin-Löf random sequences has measure 1, i.e. any randomly drawn sequence is Martin-Löf random with probability 1.

It has been shown (see [20]) that a universal Martin-Löf test U exists such that for any Martin-Löf test T, T is included in U, i.e. there is some constant c such that for all n

$$T_{n+c} \subseteq U_n ,$$

where c may depend on T. In other words, this universal test on its own is able to detect the non-randomness of any sequence, and a bit sequence $x \in \{0,1\}^\infty$ is Martin-Löf random if and only if it passes the universal test U.

Every computable sequence x can be transformed into a Martin-Löf test

$$T_x = \{(n, u) \mid u \text{ is a prefix of } x \text{ with } l(u) = n\} .$$

Now the sequence x will not pass the test T_x. This shows that no computable sequence is Martin-Löf random, analogously to the fact that such a sequence is not Kolmogorov random, since it can be described by a Turing machine of some fixed length. Actually, it was shown by Martin-Löf that the notions of Kolmogorov randomness and Martin-Löf randomness are equivalent if one considers the prefix-free version of Kolmogorov randomness (In the prefix-free

2 Different notions of (pseudo) randomness

version of Kolmogorov complexity, no description of any object can be the prefix of a description of another object).

Note that there is no efficiency requirement for these statistical tests. Thus only a very restricted version can be used in practice: Efficiently testing for randomness would be limited to a certain number of tests, and only to efficiently computable tests. With these restrictions sequences that are not Martin-Löf random might still look random to a set of efficiently computable statistical tests.

2.1.3 Martingales and predictability

Another method to look at randomness is the point of view of a gambler: Suppose a betting game where coins are thrown one after the other. A player starts with a capital of c and before each coin is thrown will bet some amount c' on the outcome of "heads" and $c - c'$ on the outcome of "tails". The player's bet on the correct outcome will be doubled, the other is lost. With a perfectly random coin, the game is fair and the expected gain is equal to 0. However, if there exists a strategy that will consistently win, then we might suspect that the sequence is not random.

Definition 11 *A martingale is a function* $m : \{0,1\}^* \to \mathbb{R}^{\geq 0}$ *with*

$$m(w) = \frac{1}{2}(m(w0) + m(w1)) \ .$$

A martingale m succeeds on an infinite sequence s if

$$\limsup_{n \to \infty} m(s_{1..n}) = \infty \ .$$

Here, the function $m(w)$ describes a player's capital after the bits of w have been thrown, $m(w0)$ is the player's capital after an additional 0, and $m(w1)$ after an additional 1. This corresponds to a betting strategy where $m(w0)/2$ is bet on a "0", and $m(w1)/2$ is bet on a "1".

It was shown by Schnorr [21] that a sequence s is Martin-Löf random iff s is not succeeded by any recursively enumerable martingale.

2.1 Notions of pseudorandomness

A martingale always has access to *all* bits of w. When restricting ourselves to martingales with a limited memory of the last k bits, then a pseudorandom generator that outputs $k+1$-wise independent numbers could not be succeeded by such a limited martingale.

Additionally, we could restrict martingales to efficiently computable functions. This leads to a slightly different view on randomness, mainly found in cryptography:

Definition 12 *Let D_n be a probability distribution on $\{0,1\}^n$ and X a random variable with $X = (X_1, \ldots, X_n) \sim D_n$. An algorithm A is an ε-predictor for D_n if for some $i < n$, it predicts X_i from $X_1, \ldots, X_{i-1}$ with probability at least $\frac{1}{2} + \varepsilon$, i.e.*

$$P[A(X_1, \ldots, X_{i-1}) = X_i] \geq \frac{1}{2} + \varepsilon \ .$$

Now if we know that a sequence of random bits is distributed according to a distribution D_n, we can use predictors to guess some bits in advance – if those predictors exist. But suppose the sequence is distributed according to the uniform distribution U_n on n-bit strings. Then no matter how we guess the outcome of an arbitrary bit of that sequence, we can only guess the correct bit with probability $\frac{1}{2}$. That is, if A is an ε-predictor for D, it behaves differently for input distributions D_n or U_n. This leads us to the next definition, that of a *distinguisher*.

Definition 13 *Let D_n and $\tilde{D}_n$ be two probability distributions on $\{0,1\}^n$, and X, Y two random variables with $X \sim D_n$ and $Y \sim \tilde{D}_n$. Then an algorithm A is an ε-distinguisher for D_n and $\tilde{D}_n$, if*

$$|P[A(X) = 1] - P[A(Y) = 1]| \geq \varepsilon \ .$$

It can be shown that an ε-distinguisher for a distribution and the uniform distribution exists if and only if an ε-predictor for that sequence exists. For a proof, see for example [22].

In cryptography, the notions of distinguishers and predictors can be used to define cryptographic security of a sequence. In this setting, a sequence (or the pseudorandom generator that produces it) is defined as cryptographically

2 Different notions of (pseudo) randomness

secure if there is no efficient distinguisher for that sequence. Here it is assumed that the seed is chosen uniformly among all possible seeds. A distinguisher is "efficient" if it runs in polynomial time, i.e. if it's contained in an efficient complexity class like BPP.

Definition 14 *A sequence of distributions $\mathcal{D} = (D_1, D_2, D_3, \ldots)$ is called a distribution ensemble, if for any $i \in \mathbb{N}$, D_i is a probability distribution on $\{0,1\}^i$. Let X_i be random variables with $X_i \sim D_i$ for all $i \in \mathbb{N}$, and let U_i denote the uniform distribution on $\{0,1\}^i$ for all $i \in \mathbb{N}$. Then the probability ensemble $\mathcal{D}$ is* cryptographically pseudorandom *if no polynomials $p(n)$ and $q(n)$ exists such that for each n there exists a $\frac{1}{q(n)}$-distinguisher for D_n and U_n with running time $p(n)$.*

Until today, it is not known if pseudorandom distribution ensembles can be efficiently generated. In cryptography, being able to generate pseudorandom sequences from smaller seeds would prove very useful: Sharing the secret seed of such a sequence would allow two parties to efficiently share the whole sequence and thus have access to a common source of bits that can't be distinguished from a source of truly random bits by any efficient algorithm.

2.1.4 Shannon Entropy

In 1948, C.E. Shannon defined a measure of randomness which was the foundation of information theory, a new scientific discipline [3]. Unlike other measures that define the randomness of single sequences, entropy measures the randomness of a stochastic process, resp. that of a random distribution.

Definition 15 *Let S be a sample space, D a probability distribution on S and X a random variable with $X \sim D$. Then*

$$H(X) := -\sum_{s \in S} P(X = s) \log_2 P(X = s)$$

is the Shannon entropy of X. The minimum entropy of X, $H_{min}(x)$, is defined as

$$H_{min}(X) := \min_{s \in S} \{-\log_2 P(X = s)\} \ .$$

2.1 Notions of pseudorandomness

Information theory also defines a measure to describe the *difference* or distance between two probability distributions: The *relative entropy* or *Kullback-Leibler distance* D between two random variables X and Y (see [24]) is defined as

$$D(X,Y) = \sum_{x \in \mathbb{R}} P(X = x) \log_2 \frac{P(X = x)}{P(Y = x)} \ .$$

For a given sample space S, we always have $0 \leq H(X) \leq \log_2 |S|$, where $H(X)$ reaches its maximum when X is uniformly distributed in S and its minimum when $P[X = s] = 1$ for an element $s \in S$.

It can be shown that Shannon entropy of a random variable $X \in S$ is a lower bound for the average code word length for any code over S. On the other hand, there always exists a code that maps every element $s \in S$ to a code word of length $\lceil -\log_2 P[X = s] \rceil$, the so-called Shannon-Fano code. Therefore, for the average codeword length $\overline{L}$ of any optimal code for S the following inequality holds:

$$H(X) \leq \overline{L} < H(X) + 1 \ .$$

Note that for any random variable X, the entropy of X cannot be increased by deterministic methods. In other words, for any function f, $H(X) \geq H(f(X))$. Therefore, the entropy of a pseudorandom sequence will never surpass the entropy of that sequence's seed. Applying a function can, however, *decrease* the entropy of a random variable, for example by mapping different values to the same value.

While Kolmogorov complexity and its equivalent notions measure the randomness of single strings, Shannon entropy measures the randomness of a probability distribution on a set of elements. But since both notions are related to the lengths of descriptions or codes of elements, there is an elegant connection between these two notions: If the probability function $p(x) := P[X = x]$ is *computable*, then

$$H(X) \leq \sum_{s \in S} P[X = s] K(s) \leq H(X) + c_p \ ,$$

where c_p is a non-negative constant that only depends on the function p. This means that Kolmogorov complexity gives us codeword lengths of a universal

2 Different notions of (pseudo) randomness

code that has almost optimal average length (up to a constant added term) for *any* distribution on the set of all strings, as long as this distribution is computable.

Note that while the Shannon entropy of a random variable X can't be increased by applying any function f to X, Kolmogorov complexity of a string x may well be increased by applying a function f to it. As long as f is computable, $f \circ p$ is still computable and the inequality above still holds, but the constant $c_{f \circ p}$ may be greater than c_p.

2.1.5 Quasi-random sequences

Algorithms following the Monte Carlo method draw many random samples from a given sample space, perform determinstic computations on these samples and then recombine the results. For example, an integral $\int_0^1 f(x)dx$ can be approximated by the sum $\frac{1}{N}\sum_{i=1}^n f(x_i)$, where $x_1, x_2, \ldots, x_N$ is a sequence of random numbers in the interval $[0,1]$ (see [25]). Since the result is largely based on the set of samples, these methods depend on a good quality of the random number generator that is used. On the other hand, due to the large number of samples needed, the random number generator should be very fast. Quasi-Monte Carlo algorithms avoid the usage of random numbers, and instead attempt to generate numbers that are spread over their domain evenly. In the case of the integral above, it can be shown that the difference between the integral and the approximating sum can be bounded from above by $V(f)D^*(x_1, \ldots, x_n)$, where $V(f)$ is the variation of f and D^* is the star discrepancy [25]. Discrepany measures how evenly a set of points in a k-dimensional cube is distributed.

Definition 16 *Let $P := \{x_1, x_2, \ldots, x_N\} \subset [0,1)^d$. Then the star discrepancy D^* of P is defined as*

$$D^*(P) := \sup_{x \in [0,1)^d} \left(\frac{|\{x_i \in P \mid \forall j. x_i^{(j)} < x^{(j)}\}|}{N} - \prod_{i=1}^d x^{(i)} \right),$$

where $x^{(j)}$ denotes the j-th component of the vector x.

2.1 Notions of pseudorandomness

Note that $\frac{|\{x_i \in P | \forall j . x_i^{(j)} < x^{(j)}\}|}{N}$ corresponds to an approximation of the volume of x when using the Monte Carlo method: For each sample, we check if the sample lies within x. At the end, we compute the fraction of these samples among the set of all samples. The expected value of our computation is then equal to the volume of x. I.e. star discrepancy measures the maximum difference between the result of this Monte Carlo computation and the correct result.

An example of a sequence with low star discrepancy is the van der Corput sequence.

Definition 17 Let $n_k, \ldots, n_0$ be the b-ary representation of a number $n \in \mathbb{N}$, such that $n = \sum_{i=0}^{k} n_i b^i$, with $0 \leq n_i < b$ for all i. We then define

$$\phi_b(n) = \sum_{j=0}^{\infty} n_i b^{-i-1} \ .$$

The van der Corput sequence *in base b is defined as*

$$X_n = \phi_b(n) \ .$$

Intuitively, ϕ_b takes the digits of a number n in b-ary representation, reverses their order and places them behind a decimal point. For example, $\phi_2(11001_2) = 0.10011_2$. A van der Corput sequence X in base b has a star discrepancy of $D_n^*(X) = O\left(\frac{\log N}{N}\right)$.

When tupels of higher dimension are needed, the van der Corput sequences can be generalized to sequences of k-tuples:

Definition 18 A Halton sequence *in the bases* $b_1, \ldots, b_k$ *is defined as*

$$X_n = (\phi_{b_1}(n), \ldots, \phi_{b_k}(n)) \ .$$

A Halton sequence is a composition of multiple van der Corput sequences with different bases. Some plots of two-dimensional Halton sequences of bases 2 and 3 can be seen in Figure 2.3. Compare with Figure 2.5, where uniformly distributed numbers were used.

2 Different notions of (pseudo) randomness

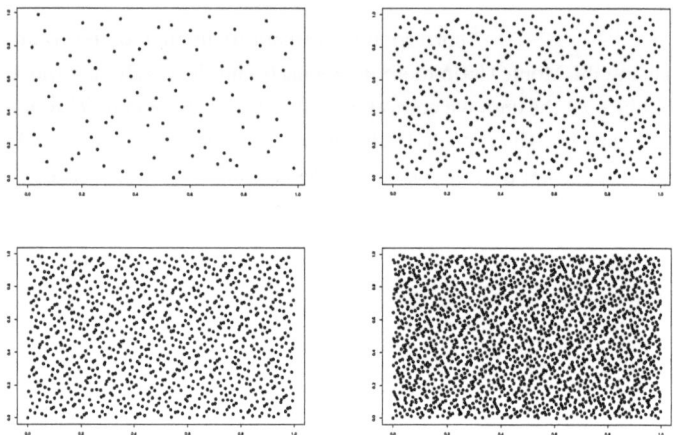

Figure 2.3: Plots of two-dimensional Halton sequences of lengths 100, 500, 1000 and 2000.

2.2 Pseudorandom Generators

A pseudorandom number generator (short PRNG) is an algorithm that outputs a new number each time it is called. Its output depends on an internal state that is changed in a deterministic way each time a number is output. A PRNG is initialized with the help of a number or sequence called the seed, which is usually chosen at random (when reproducing a result however, we might as well reuse an experiment's seed). We will call the *output* $X_0, X_1, X_2, \ldots$ of a PRNG a *pseudorandom sequence*. A pseudorandom sequence, although deterministically created, should look like a random sequence of numbers. The most common way to formalize the notion of "looking random" is via the use of statistical tests (see Section 2.1.2).

Two of the most desirable properties for pseudorandom numbers are *uniformity* (i.e. every single pseudorandom number should be distributed evenly among all possible values) and *k-wise independence* (see definition below). For these measures, we assume that the seed of the pseudorandom generator was chosen under the uniform distribution from the set of all possible seeds.

2.2 Pseudorandom Generators

Definition 19 *A sequence of random numbers $X_1, X_2, \ldots$ is k-wise independent if any subsequence $X_{i_1}, \ldots, X_{i_k}$ of length k is independent, i.e. for any $x_1, \ldots, x_k$*

$$P[X_{i_1} = x_1, \ldots, X_{i_k} = x_k] = \prod_{j=1}^{k} P[X_{i_j} = x_j] \ .$$

For $k = 2$ we call such a sequence pairwise independent.

Linear congruential generators

A *linear congruential generator* with parameters a and b, modulus m and seed $X_0 \in \{0, \ldots, m-1\}$ is defined by the recursion

$$X_{n+1} = aX_n + b \bmod m \ .$$

For further reference, see [9]. It can be shown that the parameters a and b can be shown in a way that the linear congruential generator has a period length of m. This property alone, however, does not guarantee that the resulting sequence looks random. For example, the parameters $a = b = 1$ lead to a period length of m, but not to a sequence that looks random.

Generalisations include the polynomial congruential generator, which uses a recursion of the form $X_n = \sum_{i=0}^{k} a_i x^i \bmod m$, or the inversive congruential generator, using a recursion of the form $X_n = \left(\sum_{i=0}^{k} a_i x^i \right)^{-1} \bmod m$.

Linear feedback shift registers

A linear feedback shift register is another kind congruential generator. Its binary output sequence is created by the recursion

$$x_i = \bigoplus_{j=1}^{k} a_j x_{i-j} \bmod 2 \ .$$

Such a generator can be implemented in hardware, essentially using a shift register where an internal state $(x_{i-k}, \ldots, x_{i-1})$ is stored and updated.

2 Different notions of (pseudo) randomness

Many stream ciphers used in cryptography (e.g. Trivium) are based on linear feedback shift registers. They add non-linear operations like AND and OR to make their cryptanalysis very difficult.

Explicit polynomial generators

An *explicit polynomial generator* of degree k with parameters $a_0, a_1, \ldots, a_k$ and prime m is defined by

$$X_n = \sum_{i=0}^{k} a_i n^i \bmod m \; .$$

An important property of explicit polynomial generators is k-wise independence. Within one period, any k output numbers of this generator are independent if the parameters $a_0, \ldots, a_k$ are chosen at random. The period length of such a generator is at most m, since $p(x) \equiv_m p(x+m)$ for any polynomial p. The use of this kind of generator with the QuickSort algorithm is analyzed in [12], where it is shown that 5-wise independent numbers lead to a worst case running time of $O(n \log n)$.

If only pairwise independence is needed, any class of universal hash functions can be used to create a sequence of pairwise independent numbers.

Lagged fibonacci generators

A lagged fibonacci generator produces a sequence similar to the fibonacci sequence, but it usually adds less recent numbers of the output sequence to generate a new number. A lagged fibonacci generator with parameters i_1 and i_2 and operation $\oplus$ produces the sequence defined by

$$X_n = X_{n-i_1} \oplus X_{n-i_2} \bmod m \; .$$

Typically $\oplus$ is implemented as addition, subtraction, multiplication or bitwise XOR. The seed consists of the first $\max(i_1, i_2)$ numbers of the sequence. Choosing a seed for this kind of generator is non-trivial and choosing it at random may lead to output of rather low quality. Generators of this type were used in various programs (like the mathematical software Matlab [26]), but are nowadays replaced by the Mersenne Twister. Bauke and Mertens showed in [27] that such a generator can deviate from producing the same amount of 0 and 1 bits.

Mersenne Twister

The Mersenne Twister [28] is a relatively recent pseudorandom number generator with an extremely huge period length of $2^{19937} - 1$ in the most commonly used version. It is based on a combination of linear recurrences and is currently used as the standard source of random numbers in many mathematical software projects like R [29] or Maple [30]. Any 623 subsequent numbers of its output are independent and uniformly distributed.

Isaac

Isaac (Indirection, Shift, Accumulate, Add, and Count) uses an internal state of 256 bytes and various operations to transform that internal state: Indirection (using a part of the internal state as an address inside the internal state), Shift (rotating parts of the internal state), Accumulate (accumulating a value over various iterations of the algorithm), Add and Count. It has a minimum cycle length of 2^{40} and an expected cycle length of 2^{8295}. It was designed to be cryptographically secure, and as of today, there are no efficient distinguishers or predictors known.

Cryptographic stream ciphers

Cryptographic stream ciphers are used for symmetric cryptographic protocols where both partners need the same key. Instead of exchanging a long binary sequence, only the seed of a stream cipher is exchanged, which is then used to create a long bit sequence. Trivium, for example, is a stream cipher that was constructed to be cryptographically secure and easy to implement both in hardware as in software [31]. It is based on three feedback shift registers of

2 Different notions of (pseudo) randomness

lengths 93, 84 and 111. In each step, its internal state changes as follows:

$$(a_1, a_2, \ldots, a_{93}) \leftarrow (c_{66} \oplus c_{111} \oplus c_{109} \wedge c_{110} \oplus a_{69}, a_1, \ldots, a_{92})$$
$$(b_1, b_2, \ldots, b_{84}) \leftarrow (a_{66} \oplus a_{93} \oplus a_{91} \wedge a_{92} \oplus b_{78}, b_1, \ldots, b_{83})$$
$$(c_1, c_2, \ldots, c_{111}) \leftarrow (b_{69} \oplus b_{84} \oplus b_{82} \wedge b_{83} \oplus c_{87}, c_1, \ldots, c_{110}) \ .$$

The output of each step is $a_{66} \oplus a_{93} \oplus b_{69} \oplus b_{84} \oplus c_{66} \oplus c_{111}$. As of July 2009, no attack on Trivium is known that is faster than a brute-force attack.

Physical random sources

Instead of using a small seed to produce many numbers, one could also think of ways to rapidly "capture" randomness from physical processes. A few physical sources have already been used to obtain random numbers:

- Radio frequencies where no signal is broadcast contains only atmospheric noise, which is mainly caused by lightnings all over the world. This noise can be measured with the help of a radio antenna and transformed into a sequence of random numbers.
- When a beam of photons is sent through a so-called beam splitter, every photon has two possible paths to leave that beam splitter. By using fast detectors that can detect single photons, this method can produce random bits at a rate of about 1 Mbit/s [32, 33].

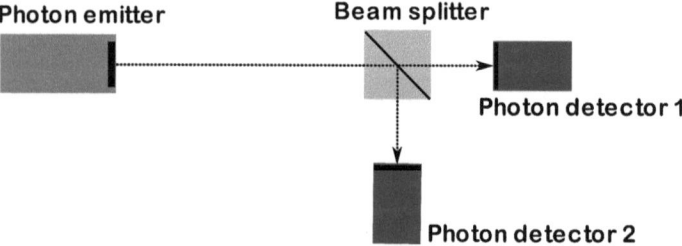

Figure 2.4: Creating random bits with a beam splitter. Photons are emitted by the photon emitter. With probability 0.5 they pass the beam splitter and are reported by detector 0. With probability 0.5 they are reflected by the beam splitter and are then reported by detector 1.

Archived bits

Instead of using a given pseudorandom generator, one can instead use random bits that are available on CD, DVD or the internet. This idea isn't new, however: Back in 1927, a book with the title "Random sampling numbers" was published, containing mostly tables of random numbers [34].

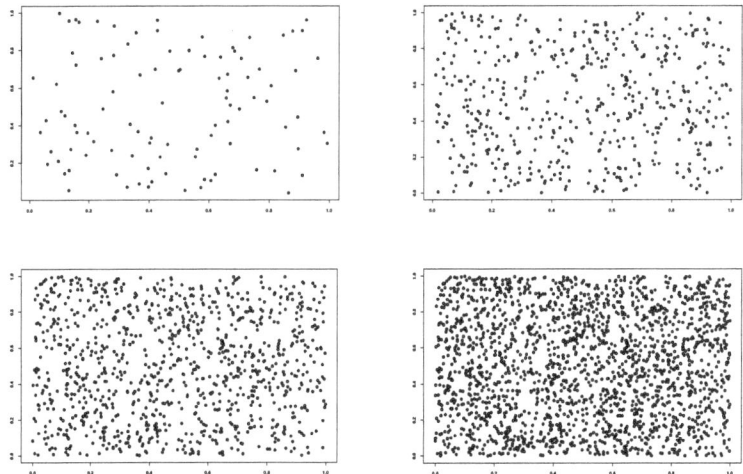

Figure 2.5: Some sets of random two-dimensional points. Set sizes are 100, 500, 1000 and 2000. The numbers are from Marsaglia's Diehard sequence [35].

Marsaglia's Diehard suite [35] is one of these sources available on the internet. It is a set of statistical tests that was published on CDROM in 1995, along with several files of bit sequences that pass these tests. These sequences were obtained by the bitwise XOR of several sequences, some of them obtained from physical devices, some of them from other sources like pseudorandom number generators or even an audio CD. This approach is based on the following fact: Let $X, Y \in \{0, 1\}$ be two independent random variables. Then $X \oplus Y$ is *uniformly* distributed if at least one of the two variables is uniformly distributed. This way, the bitwise XOR of several sequences is uniformly distributed among the set of all bit sequences of the same length, if at least one of those sequences was uniformly distributed. Thus, one could hope to obtain a good pseudorandom

2 Different notions of (pseudo) randomness

sequence when forming the bitwise XOR of several sequences that are supposed to behave like true random numbers. For some plots of numbers from this source, see Figure 2.5.

Another source of random bits is the web page random.org [36]. It measures atmospheric noise and converts it into random bits. Right now, everybody can download a limited amount of random bits from that source for free.

The δ-random source

A general model of a random bit source is the δ-random-source, which is sometimes also referred to as *slightly random source*. It models a source of random bits that are neither independent nor uniformly distributed. Since the bias of each bit is a function of the previous output, it can be applied as an adversary argument and is particularly suited for worst-case analysis. See also [37, 38, 39, 14, 40].

Definition 20 (See [39]) *A δ-random-source is a random bit generator. Its bias may depend on the bits it has previously output, but the probability to output "1" must be in the range $[\delta, 1-\delta]$. Therefore, it has an internal state $\omega \in \{0,1\}^*$, denoting its previously output bits.*

To obtain a random number X in the range $1, \ldots, n$ from the δ-random-source, we output $\lceil \log n \rceil$ bits and interpret them as a number Y. Then, we set $X := (Y \bmod n) + 1$.

Note that in contrast to a pseudorandom generator, the δ-random source's output doesn't have a limited amount of entropy: While the entropy of any pseudorandom generator is bounded by the entropy of the seed (i.e. usually the length of the seed), the entropy of the δ-random source's output is at least $H(\delta, 1-\delta)$ *per bit*, where H is the entropy function. This stems from the fact that the conditional entropy of each new bit is at least $H(\delta, 1-\delta)$, no matter what the previous output looks like.

2.3 Influence on Algorithms

Pseudorandom numbers are used in various algorithms. For some algorithms, theoretical and empirical results are known about the influence of different pseudorandom generators on the results of these algorithms.

In [15, 16], a simple evolutionary algorithm was run with various pseudorandom generators, but no direct connection between the "quality" of the random generator and the quality of the solution was found. This indicates that the given evolutionary algorithm does not depend on a very high quality of the random numbers involved, resp. that it is hard to find a good measure of quality. In Chapter 5, we will examine different aspects for describing the quality of the randomness and its implications on the solution of the heuristics.

Simulated Annealing, another search heuristic, is severely influenced by the period length of the pseudorandom generator. In Chapter 5, we will examine the influence of random sources with limited randomness on the solution for the Traveling Salesman problem, among others, solved with the Simulated Annealing heuristic. Part of this work has been published in [41].

It is a well-known fact that Shannon's entropy is a lower bound for any sorting method that is based on pairwise comparisons. The entropy of a uniform distribution on the set of all permutations of n elements is equal to $\log_2(n!) = \Theta(n \log n)$. For the randomized version of the QuickSort algorithm, some additional results have been achieved. Karloff et al. [12] showed that QuickSort's worst case complexity can go up to $\Omega(n^2)$ when sorting n numbers with the help of a linear congruential generator. They also showed that QuickSort shows an average case running time of $O(n \log n)$ when using an explicit polynomial generator of degree 4. Their main argument uses the fact that this generator produces 5-wise independent numbers. B. List et al. [14, 40] showed how QuickSort's running time is gradually increased to $\Omega(n^2)$ when the probability of "bad" pivot elements (i.e. very small or large elements) increases.

Chor and Golreich have shown that k-wise independent random numbers are a useful tool for sampling [42]. With this method, only the random bits for a seed are needed and the chance of hitting any subset of the sample space is still good. This can be used to reduce the error probability of RP algorithms with

2 Different notions of (pseudo) randomness

relatively few bits. Usually, such an algorithm's error probability can be reduced by running it multiple times, each time using *new* random numbers. The use of k-wise independent bits allows the same technique to some lesser degree: If the algorithm needs r random bits, these r bits can be used as a seed for a pseudorandom number generator that creates k-wise independent bits for some k. The algorithm can then be run multiple times, using bits from the pseudo random generator. Repeating the algorithm l times, the error probability can be reduced to $O(1/l)$, while still only r bits were used. This approach can also be used for BPP algorithms. Note that using true random bits would reduce the error probability exponentially in l, at the cost of a total of lr random bits. Further uses of pairwise independent numbers can be found in an overview of M. Luby and A. Wigderson [43].

Bach [13] showed that linear congruential generators with a prime modulus are a sufficient source of randomness for computing square roots modulo a prime p (with two probabilistic algorithms from Lehmer [44] and Shanks [45]), for computing q-th roots modulo a prime p (with a probabilistic algorithm by Adleman, Manders and Miller [46]), and for testing primality (with the Miller test [47]). For each of these algorithms, the error probability was shown to not increase when a linear congruential generator was used instead of independent, uniformly distributed random numbers.

Hoos et. al. [17] empirically examined the influence of some pseudorandom generators on the result of probabilistic algorithms for the satisfiability problem. They observed that the quality of the random numbers didn't influence the output quality of these algorithms. However, completely derandomizing the algorithms caused them to fail for a few input instances and made parallelization difficult.

Azar et. al. [48] show that random walks can be influenced by a biased source of randomness. They consider random walks on d-regular graphs (i.e. graphs where every node has degree d) and a random source that outputs values $1, 2, \ldots, d$. At each step, with probability $1 - \varepsilon$, that number is drawn randomly under a uniform distribution. With probability ε, a deterministic process may decide which number is output. They show that the limit probability of any subset $S \subseteq V$ of the graph's vertices can be raised from $|S|/|V|$ to $(|S|/|V|)^{1-c\varepsilon}$.

2.3 Influence on Algorithms

This result also shows that a biased random source could decrease a Markov chain's probability to converge to a good solution.

The rho algorithm for factoring numbers is based on the birthday paradox, a statistical fact about independent random numbers. In and of itself, this approach would not be able to beat the running time of the naive approach. The rho algortihm however exploits the fact that it uses a pseudorandom generator. It uses the regularity of that pseudorandom generator to save many computations and thus achieves a much better running time.

2 Different notions of (pseudo) randomness

3 Algorithms and non-perfect randomness

In this chapter, we will investigate probabilistic algorithms and prove some implications that arise from the usage of non-perfect randomness. In Section 3.1 we will start with an equality test for polynomials (or multi-sets) and show that the most common type of pseudorandom generator is not suited to decrease the algorithm's running time via repetitions. Section 3.2 will consider Karger's probabilistic algorithm for calculating the minimum cut of a graph. Here we will show how the algorithm can be adapted to a source that is biased towards leading to malevolent random choices, with a slight increase in running time. In Section 3.3, we will show how a biased random source increases the error probability of Schöning's random walk algorithm for the Boolean Satisfiability Problem. This algorithm is influenced by the choice of the initial assignment to the input formula as well as by the random choices that are made during the random walk.

3.1 Testing the equality of polynomials

Testing the equality of polynomials is a nice example that shows the power of randomness – the algorithm doesn't do much more than draw a random number and evaluate and compare two polynomials at that value, then repeat that process several times. Still, it's among the fastest known methods for that problem. With pseudorandom numbers, however, the algorithm might work much worse. We will give a short introduction to the basic algorithms for testing the equality of polynomials and show how the use of pseudorandom numbers can lead to significantly worse results than the use of truly random numbers.

3 Algorithms and non-perfect randomness

Consider the task of testing if two polynomials

$$a(x) = \prod_{i=0}^{n}(x - a_i) \quad \text{and} \quad b(x) = \prod_{i=0}^{n}(x - b_i)$$

are identical. Note that this task is equivalent to testing the equality of the two multisets $A = \{a_0, \ldots, a_n\}$ and $B = \{b_0, \ldots, b_n\}$. A standard deterministic approach could be the following: Sort both sets of coefficients (a_i) and (b_i); then check if the sorted sequences are equal. This approach has an expected running time of $O(n \log n)$.

There exists a randomized approach that is faster (see [49, 18]), with a running time in $O(n)$: Evaluate the two polynomials at a random position x_0 (see Alg. 1) and compare the two values.

Input: Two polynomials $a(x)$ and $b(x)$ of degree n
Output: "equal" if $a \equiv b$; "not equal" if $a \not\equiv b$.
// m should be a prime with $m \gg n$ and $\forall i : m > a_i, b_i$
Choose x_0 uniformly from $\{0, \ldots, m-1\}$;
if $a(x_0) \neq b(x_0) \pmod{m}$ **then**
    return "not equal";
else
    return "equal";
end

Algorithm 1: Probabilistic equality test

If a and b are identical, the algorithm never errs. If a and b are not equal, there is a small probability that the algorithm gives the wrong result: If x_0 is a root of the polynomial $c(x) := a(x) - b(x) \bmod m$, the algorithm errs. Since c is of degree at most n, there are at most n different roots and thus the probability of error is at most n/m. Note that this method even works if one of the polynomials is given in the form $a(x) = \sum_{i=0}^{n} \tilde{a}_i x^i$.

To avoid computing with a large modulus m, we could use a smaller m but repeat the algorithm several times (see Alg. 2).

3.1 Testing the equality of polynomials

Input: Two polynomials $a(x)$ and $b(x)$ of degree n
Output: "equal" if $a \equiv b$; "not equal" if $a \not\equiv b$.
`// Now, m should be a prime with m > 2n and ∀i : m > aᵢ,bᵢ`
for $i=1$ **to** t **do**
    Choose x_i uniformly from $\{0,\ldots,m-1\}$;
    if $a(x_i) \neq b(x_i) \pmod{m}$ **then** return "not equal"
end
return "equal";

Algorithm 2: Slightly improved version of Alg. 1

In Algorithm 2, each of the t iterations has error probability at most n/m. Using independently drawn x_i, we achieve an error probability of at most $(n/m)^t$. Since $n/m < \frac{1}{2}$, this results in an error probability of at most 2^{-t}. We will now show that using a certain type of pseudorandom number generator, we might not be able to decrease the error probability exponentially. We will even show that repeating the evaluation of the polynomials with the help of a linear congruential generator only results in a negligible decrease of the error probability.

Theorem 3.1 *Let G be a pseudorandom number generator that has the following properties:*

1. *G uses a recurrence of the form*

$$X_{i+1} = f(X_i) \bmod m$$

   to produce its output $X_1, X_2, \ldots$.

2. *G has period length m for every possible seed.*

Then if G is used as the source of randomness, Algorithm 2 has error probability

$$p_{\text{err}} = \frac{n-t+1}{m}$$

for some worst case input $a(x)$ and $b(x)$.

Proof. Fix one seed X_1 given to G. Let $X_1, X_2, \ldots, X_n$ be the first n numbers output by G. Let $c := \prod_{i=1}^{n}(x - X_i)$ and choose two polynomials $a(x)$ and $b(x)$ such that $c(x) = a(x) - b(x)$. Note that a and b are different (w.l.o.g. we assume that at

3 Algorithms and non-perfect randomness

least one of the pseudorandom numbers is non-zero). Now, with seed X_i, Alg. 2 only evaluates $a(x)$ and $b(x)$ at positions $X_i, \ldots, X_{i+t-1}$, which are all roots of c if $1 \leq i \leq n-t+1$. Thus, the algorithm gives a wrong output for $n-t+1$ out of m seeds. When the seed is chosen uniformly from $\{0, \ldots, m-1\}$, this results in an error probability of $(n-t+1)/m$. ∎

Note that our theorem is also applicable to generators that use a recurrence of the form $Y_{i+1} = f(Y_i)$ for their internal state Y, mapping that internal state to the output X with another function, i.e. $X_i = g(Y_i)$.

Also note that our proof relies on the fact that different seeds for G lead to similar output sequences: The suffix of one pseudorandom sequence can be created by simply using a different seed. Linear congruential generators and linear feedback shift registers show this property, for example. Different kinds of pseudorandom generators where two sequences generated from different seeds do not share long common subsequences might still be useful for decreasing the error probability of Alg. 2.

At first glance, the explicit polynomial generator (see [50]; for a definition, see Section 2.2) looks like a good candidate to circumvent this situation, due to the independence of its output:

Lemma 3.1 *When using a polynomial generator with degree $k = t$ and modulus $m = p$ for a prime p, Alg. 2 has error probability at most $(n/m)^t$.*

Proof. The lemma follows directly from the properties of the polynomial generator:

1. For each i, X_i is uniformly distributed in $\{0, \ldots, m-1\}$.
2. The output is $k-wise$ independent, i.e. any subset of $\{X_0, X_1, \ldots\}$ of size k is independent. In other words, the conditional distribution of an output position X_{i_k} is still uniform when $X_{i_1}, \ldots, X_{i_{k-1}}$ are known.

That way, the probability that X_i is a root of the difference polynomial is at most n/m. Since $X_1, \ldots, X_t$ are independent, the probability that they are all roots of the difference polynomial is not greater than $(n/m)^t$. ∎

3.1 Testing the equality of polynomials

Note that this lemma still doesn't give us an advantage in practice: The size of the seed is so large that we could use it directly as our random sequence. An explicit polynomial generator with degree k *smaller* than t might at least improve the bound of Theorem 3.1.

Lemma 3.2 *When using a polynomial generator with parameters $k < t$ and $m = p$, Algorithm 2 has error probability at least $(n-t+1)/m^k$ and at most $(n/m)^k$.*

Proof. Our proof for the lower bound is similar to that of Theorem 3.1. Fix a given seed $a_0, \ldots, a_k$. The output of the polynomial generator is the sequence $f(0), f(1), f(2), \ldots$ with $f(x) = \sum_{i=0}^{k} a_i x^i$. Now construct an input $a(x), b(x)$ where $a(x) - b(x)$ has roots $f(0), f(1), \ldots, f(n-1)$. That way, Alg. 2 errs because it evaluates the polynomials at the first t roots of $a-b$. We note that Alg. 2 also errs when it gets $f(i), f(i+1), \ldots, f(i+k-1)$ as random numbers, with $0 \leq i \leq n-t$. This means that the algorithm also errs when the seed consists of the coefficients of the polynomial $f(x+i)$. It follows that there are at least $n-t+1$ seeds that lead to a wrong answer for the input $a(x), b(x)$.

For the upper bound we use the same properties as in Lemma 3.1: The first k pseudorandom numbers are uniformly distributed and independent, so each number has only a chance of at most n/m to be a root of $a-b$. Since $t > m$, this leads to a total error probability of at most $(n/m)^k$. ∎

So while the error probability of Algorithm 2 decreases exponentially for the first k repetitions (where k is the degree of the polynomial generator), any further repetitions might still decrease the error probability only linearly in the number of additional repetitions. One solution for this problem might be pseudorandom generators where different seeds lead to different output sequences that are *not* shifted versions of each other. To this end, a special form of hashing might lead to a solution. Note however, that even universal hash classes, a common family of hash functions that is considered useful in the standard context of hashing, only leads to pairwise independent numbers.

3 Algorithms and non-perfect randomness

3.2 Karger's algorithm for the minimum cut

Karger's algorithm (see [51]) for computing the minimum cut of a graph is another good example where randomness is used in a simple yet elegant way to solve a combinatoric problem.

Definition 21 *A cut of a connected (multi)-graph $G = (V, E)$ is a set $E' \subseteq E$ such that the graph $G = (V, E \setminus E')$ is unconnected. A minimum cut of G is a cut of minimal size.*

In order to find a minimum cut, Karger's algorithm uses the fact that, with rather high probability, choosing an edge at random will select an edge that is not part of the minimum cut. The two vertices that are connected by the chosen edge are then collapsed into one vertex. If the edge was not part of the minimum cut, collapsing the two vertices preserves the minimum cut, so the algorithm can repeat this process until only two vertices are left. Pseudocode is shown in Algorithm 3.

Input: (Multi-)Graph $G = (V, E)$.
Output: Set of all edges belonging to the minimum cut of G.
while *G has more than 2 nodes* **do**
    Choose an edge $e = \{u, v\} \in E$ at random;
    Delete all edges between u and v from E;
    Combine u and v into one vertex;
end
Output E;

Algorithm 3: RandomizedMinCut

Let $n := |V|$. The algorithm needs to run the while loop $n - 2$ times. During the i-th run, a subset of the minimum cut is removed with probability at most $\frac{2}{n-i+1}$, under the condition that the minimum cut was still present at the beginning of that run. The minimum cut is output at the end if it hasn't been eliminated during the run of the algorithm. This leads to a success probability of $\Omega(1/n^2)$. To make the error probability sufficiently small, the algorithm is run $O(n^2)$ times. Since each run has a complexity of $O(n^2)$ steps, the overall running time is $O(n^4)$.

3.2 Karger's algorithm for the minimum cut

Input: (Multi-)Graph $G = (V, E)$.
Output: Set of all edges belonging to the minimum cut of G.
while G has more than $n/\sqrt{2}$ nodes **do**
    Choose an edge $e = \{u, v\} \in E$ at random;
    Delete all edges between u and v from E;
    Combine u and v into one vertex;
end
$E_1 \leftarrow$ RecursiveMinCut(G);
$E_2 \leftarrow$ RecursiveMinCut(G);
if $|E_1| < |E_2|$ **then**
    Output E_1;
else
    Output E_2;
end

Algorithm 4: RecursiveMinCut, the improved version of Algorithm 3.

An improved version of the algorithm uses the fact that the probability of eliminating the minimum cut is very low at the beginning, but rises with each step of the algorithm: While the number of edges belonging to the minimum cut remains constant, the total number of edges in the graph continually decreases. Thus, the improved version runs until only a fraction of $1/\sqrt{2}$ of the original number of nodes is left. Then, the algorithm is run recursively *twice* on the remaining graph. The best of the two solutions is returned. The fraction $1/\sqrt{2}$ is chosen because when that many vertices are left, the probability that the minimum cut survived so far is still about $1/2$. Thus for a graph with n vertices, the success probability can be formulated recursively as

$$p(n) = \frac{1}{2}\left(1 - \left(1 - p\left(n/\sqrt{2}\right)\right)^2\right),$$

which leads to a success probability of $\Omega\left(\frac{1}{\log n}\right)$. A single run of the algorithm has a running time of $O(n^2 \log n)$, so the total running time, with $O(\log n)$ repetitions, is $O(n^2 \log^2 n)$. For more details, we refer the reader to [18].

The run-time analysis of this algorithm assumes the availability of uniformly distributed, independent random numbers that can be utilized to choose the edges. We now consider a source of randomness that is biased towards choosing an edge belonging to the minimum cut. Let E_c be the set of the edges in the

3 Algorithms and non-perfect randomness

minimum cut. (Note that for simplicity's sake, we will assume that there is only one unique minimum cut in the graph, calling it *the* minimum cut.) Then we will assume that the probability that our random source chooses any edge in E_c is d times as high as the probability that it chooses any edge in $E \setminus E_c$, for some constant $d > 1$. In other words,

$$P(e) = \begin{cases} \frac{d}{|E|+(d-1)|E_c|} & \text{if } e \in E_c \\ \frac{1}{|E|+(d-1)|E_c|} & \text{if } e \in E_0 \end{cases}.$$

Since the set of edges of the graph shrinks during the run of the algorithm, we will formally have to deal with several different probability distributions. Therefore, we define the notion of a probability set with bias:

Definition 22 Let $G = (V, E)$ be a multigraph and $E_c \subseteq E$ a multiset of edges. A probability set for G with bias d towards E_c is a set of probability distributions $\{P_S \mid S \subseteq E\}$ such that P_S is a probability distribution on S with

$$P_S(e) = \begin{cases} \frac{d}{|S|+(d-1)|E_c \cap S|} & \text{if } e \in E_c \\ \frac{1}{|S|+(d-1)|E_c \cap S|} & \text{if } e \in S \setminus E_c \end{cases}.$$

Note that the probability distributions in such a set have relatively high entropy, even for rather large values of d. For $|S| = n$ and $|E_c \cap S| = k$, the entropy of P_S amounts to

$$\begin{aligned}
H(P_S) \\
&= -k \frac{d}{n+(d-1)k} \log \frac{d}{n+(d-1)k} - (n-k) \frac{1}{n+(d-1)k} \log \frac{1}{n+(d-1)k} \\
&= -k \frac{d \log d}{n+(d-1)k} + k \frac{d \log(n+(d-1)k)}{n+(d-1)k} + \frac{n-k}{n+(d-1)k} \log(n+(d-1)k) \\
&= \log(n+(d-1)k) - \frac{kd \log d}{n+(d-1)k} \\
&\geq \log(n+(d-1)k) - \log d \\
&\geq \log n - \log d .
\end{aligned}$$

For example, with a bias of 2, the probability that any individual edge in E_c is chosen is twice as high as the probability that any individual edge not in E_c is

3.2 Karger's algorithm for the minimum cut

chosen. This results in a distribution with entropy at least $(\log n) - 1$, where n is the total number of edges.

We will first analyze the success probability of the simpler version, Alg. 3. Let $n = |V|$ be the number of vertices in G. Assume that $|E_c| = k$, i.e. the size of the minimum cut is k. At the beginning of the i-th iteration of the while loop, each node has degree at least k and there are $n + 1 - i$ nodes left, so the graph has at least $\frac{(n+1-i)k}{2}$ edges. Drawing an edge from E with our biased random source, we draw an edge of the minimum cut with probability $\frac{kd}{\frac{(n+1-i)k}{2} + (d-1)k}$. The probability that the minimum cut survives all $n - 2$ steps is then

$$\prod_{i=1}^{n-2} \left(1 - \frac{kd}{\frac{(n+1-i)k}{2} + (d-1)k}\right)$$
$$= \prod_{i=1}^{n-2} \left(1 - \frac{2d}{(n+1-i) + 2(d-1)}\right)$$
$$= \prod_{i=1}^{n-2} \frac{n-1-i}{n-1-i+2d}$$
$$= \prod_{i=1}^{n-2} \frac{i}{i+2d} = \Theta\left(\frac{1}{n^{2d}}\right),$$

where we use Lemma 1.1. For $d \approx 1$, this error probability is not far from the $\Theta(n^{-2})$ that we get when using uniformly distributed random numbers. But note that if the algorithm is repeated only cn^2 times, the error probability is then approximately

$$p_{\text{err}} \approx \left(1 - \frac{1}{n^{2d}}\right)^{cn^2} = \left(1 - \frac{1}{n^{2d}}\right)^{n^{2d} cn^2 / n^{2d}} \approx e^{-cn^{2-2d}},$$

a term that converges to 1 for $n \to \infty$, as soon as $d > 1$.

We now analyze the improved version of the algorithm. Running the algorithm for $n - \frac{n}{\sqrt{2}}$ steps usually leads to an error probability of $\frac{1}{2}$. In the case of our biased random source, however, we get a success probability of

$$\prod_{i=1}^{n-n/\sqrt{2}} \frac{n-i-1}{n-i-1+2d} = \prod_{i=n/\sqrt{2}-1}^{n-2} \frac{i}{i+2d} \approx \frac{1}{2^d}$$

3 Algorithms and non-perfect randomness

(see the notes after Lemma 1.1). In order to raise this success probability up to $\frac{1}{2}$, we have to decrease the number of steps: With a bias of d, we should run the algorithm only until $n/\sqrt[2d]{n}$ vertices remain. That way, the error probability is

$$\prod_{i=1}^{n-n/\sqrt[2d]{2}} \frac{n-i-1}{n-i-1+2d} = \prod_{i=n/\sqrt[2d]{2}-1}^{n-2} \frac{i}{i+2d} \approx \left(\frac{1}{\sqrt[2d]{2}}\right)^{2d} = \frac{1}{2} .$$

Now the running time $T(n)$ can be described by the recursion

$$T(n) = 2T(n/\sqrt[2d]{2}) + O(n^2) .$$

By means of the Master Theorem (Theorem 1.1), we can compute the solution

$$T(n) = \Theta(n^{2d}) .$$

With our modification, a single run has a success probability of at least $\frac{1}{2d\log n}$, which we will show by induction. For the success probability $p(n)$ on a graph with n vertices, the following recursion holds:

$$\begin{aligned}
p(n) &\geq \frac{1}{2}\left(1 - \left(1 - p(n/\sqrt[2d]{2})\right)^2\right) \\
&= \frac{1}{2}\left(2p(n/\sqrt[2d]{2}) - p(n/\sqrt[2d]{2})^2\right) \\
&\geq \frac{1}{2d\log\left(\frac{n}{\sqrt[2d]{2}}\right)} - \frac{1/2}{\left(2d\log\left(\frac{n}{\sqrt[2d]{2}}\right)\right)^2} \\
&= \frac{2d\log n - 1.5}{(2d\log n - 1)^2} \\
&\geq \frac{1}{2d\log n} .
\end{aligned}$$

The results of our calculations are summed up in the following theorem:

Theorem 3.2 *Given a graph $G = (V, E)$ with a minimum cut E_c. Assume that the edges of E are randomly selected via a probability set for G with bias d towards E_c (see Definition 22). Then there is a modification of Algorithm 3 that finds the minimum cut of any graph G in running time $O(n^{2+2d})$ if that probability set is used to randomly*

3.3 Schöning's random walk algorithm for the Boolean Satisfiability Problem

select the edges. There is a modification of Algorithm 4 that finds the minimum cut in $O(n^{2d} \log n)$ steps when using that probability set.

Proof. See the calculations above. ∎

3.3 Schöning's random walk algorithm for the Boolean Satisfiability Problem

The Boolean Satisfiability Problem (short: SAT) is a well-known NP-complete decision problem that is sometimes referred to as the "drosophila of complexity theory" because of its universal character – many problems can be easily expressed as a Boolean formula. It is one of the first problems that have been shown to be NP-complete (cf. [52]).

The input, a Boolean formula, is based on a number of variables $x_1, \ldots, x_n$. A literal is a variable x_i or the negation of a variable $\neg x_i$. In the most common formulation of SAT, the formula has to be given in conjunctive normal form. In this case, the formula consists of several clauses $C_1, C_2, \ldots, C_m$, where each clause is a set of literals. An assignment $a = (a_1, a_2, \ldots, a_n) \in \{0,1\}^n$ provides a value for each literal. a_i is the value assigned to x_i, while $1 - a_i$ is assigned to a negative literal $\neg x_i$. A clause C evaluates to true under the assignment a if a assigns 1 to at least one of the literals in C. F evaluates to 1 under a if all clauses of F are evaluated to 1. In that case, we also say that a satisfies F. If such an a exists, F is satisfiable. Otherwise, F is unsatisfiable. The Boolean Satisfiability Problem consists of all satisfiable formulas. We can also formulate it as a decision problem: Given a Boolean formula F, is F satisfiable? If the size of the clauses of F is limited to k, the problem is called k-SAT. For $k \geq 3$, k-SAT is NP-complete.

Example. Define two formulas based on the variables x_1, x_2, x_3 and x_4:

$$F_1 := \{\{x_1, x_2, \neg x_3\}, \{\neg x_1, \neg x_3, x_4\}, \{x_1, \neg x_2, \neg x_4\}, \{\neg x_1, x_2, x_3\}\},$$
$$F_2 := \{\{x_1, x_2\}, \{\neg x_2\}, \{\neg x_1, x_3\}, \{\neg x_1, x_2, \neg x_3\}\}$$

3 Algorithms and non-perfect randomness

Both F_1 and F_2 are 3-SAT formulas. F_1 is satisfiable, with $a = (1,1,0,1)$ being a satisfying assignment. F_2 is not satisfiable.

A SAT algorithm with one of the best known theoretically proven running times, Schöning's random walk algorithm [53], is shown in Alg. 5. Starting with a random assignment a, as long as that assignment does not satisfy the input formula F, a is modified, one bit at a time, until a satisfying assignment is found or a certain number of modifications has been performed. If no satisfying assignment is found, the formula is assumed to be unsatisfiable. For each of the modifications, only those variables are considered that are found in a so-called null clause, a clause that is not satisfied by a. This way, each modification has the chance to flip one value of the current assignment a to the correct position.

Input: A Boolean Formula F with n variables.
Output: "yes" if F is satisfiable; "no" if it's not.
$a \leftarrow$ random assignment in $\{0,1\}^n$;
for $i=1$ **to** $3n$ **do**
    if a *satisfies* F **then**
        return "satisfiable";
    end
    Choose a clause C that is not satisfied by a;
    Randomly choose a variable in C and invert its value in a;
end
return "not satisfiable";

Algorithm 5: Schöning's random walk algorithm for the Boolean Satisfiability Problem.

If the input formula F is not satisfiable, the algorithm always gives the correct output. However, if F is satisfiable, the algorithm may fail to find a satisfying assignment and give an incorrect answer. This error probability can be reduced by running the algorithm several times. If at least one of these runs finds a satisfying assignment, the formula can be considered satisfiable. When using independent, uniformly distributed random numbers for the choice of the variable to be flipped, this algorithm has an error probability of at most $((1+\frac{1}{k-1})/2)^n$, where k is the maximal size of the clauses in F. For 3-SAT, this results in an error probability of $\left(\frac{3}{4}\right)^n$. Repeating the algorithm $20 \cdot \left(\frac{4}{3}\right)^n$ times

3.3 Schöning's random walk algorithm for the Boolean Satisfiability Problem

reduces the probability to not find a satisfying assignment to a negligibly small number.

We will now show how a bias in the random generator can increase the error probability for the 3-SAT case. Assume that the formula F has only one satisfying assignment and that F is a worst case formula in the sense that the satisfying assignment assigns the value 1 to exactly one literal in each clause of F. We further assume that our random source has a bias towards pointing to the wrong variable, i.e. it only gives the correct variable with probability $\frac{1}{3} - \delta$ instead of $\frac{1}{3}$. That way, each "flip" of a bit in the assignment reduces the Hamming distance to the solution by 1 with probability $\frac{1}{3} - \delta$, and increases it by 1 with probability $2/3 - \delta$. Note that this is a slight generalization of the δ-random source described in Section 2.2. Now assume that α^j is the probability that the algorithm finds the satisfying assignment if the initial assignment a has j incorrect bits. This leads to the recursion

$$\alpha^j = \left(\frac{1}{3} - \delta\right)\alpha^{j-1} + \left(\frac{2}{3} + \delta\right)\alpha^{j+1}$$

and thus

$$0 = \left(\frac{2}{3} + \delta\right)\alpha^2 - \alpha + \left(\frac{1}{3} - \delta\right).$$

One solution to this equation is $\alpha = 1$ (which is not the solution we are looking for), and dividing by $1 - \alpha$ leads to $0 = (2 + 3\delta)\alpha - (1 - 3\delta)$ or

$$\alpha = \frac{1 - 3\delta}{2 + 3\delta}.$$

Since there are $\binom{n}{j}$ possible start assignments with j incorrect bits, the total error probability then averages to

$$2^{-n}\sum_{j=0}^{n}\binom{n}{j}\alpha^j = \left(\frac{1+\alpha}{2}\right)^n = \left(\frac{1 + \frac{1-3\delta}{2+3\delta}}{2}\right)^n = \left(\frac{3}{4 + 6\delta}\right)^n.$$

In addition to the biased source for selecting a variable to flip, the random source used to find an initial assignment may also be biased. Assume that for each variable x_i, its initial assignment a_i is set to the incorrect value with probability

55

3 Algorithms and non-perfect randomness

$\frac{1}{2}+\varepsilon$. Then the average error probability sums up to

$$\sum_{j=0}^{n}\binom{n}{j}\left(\frac{1}{2}+\varepsilon\right)^{j}\left(\frac{1}{2}-\varepsilon\right)^{(n-j)}\alpha^{j} = \left(\left(\frac{1}{2}+\varepsilon\right)\alpha+\left(\frac{1}{2}-\varepsilon\right)\right)^{n}$$
$$= \left(\frac{1+\alpha}{2}-\varepsilon(1-\alpha)\right)^{n}.$$

Substituting α, we get an error probability of

$$\left(\frac{3-2\varepsilon(1+6\delta)}{4+6\delta}\right)^{n},$$

compared to $\left(\frac{3}{4}\right)^{n}$ when using non-biased random numbers.

Note that we used a few simplifications in order to make the calculation easier: The random process we considered did not stop after $3n$ steps, and we did not consider the "reflecting end" of the random process, i.e. the fact that the assignment a can never have more than n incorrect bits. We will take these into account in the formal proof below, which will also cover the more general case of a k-SAT formula.

Theorem 3.3 *Assume that the random walk algorithm for SAT (Algorithm 5) always chooses the first null-clause found in the formula. Let $S' = (S'_1, S'_2, S'_3, \ldots)$ be a sequence of biased random variables in $\{0,1\}$ with probability $P(S'_i = 0) = \frac{1}{2}+\varepsilon$ for all $i \geq 1$. Let $S = (S_1, S_2, S_3, \ldots)$ be a sequence of biased random variables in $\{1, \ldots, k\}$ with probabilities $P(S_i = 1) = \frac{1}{k} - \delta$ and $P(S_i \in \{2,3\}) = \frac{k-1}{k} + \delta$ for all $i \geq 1$. Then, the algorithm has a worst case error probability of*

$$p(n)\left(\frac{k-2\varepsilon(k-2+2\delta k)}{2k-2+2\delta k}\right)^{n}$$

for a polynomial p if it uses S' for selecting the initial assignment and S for the choice of the variable that is flipped.

Proof. The proof for the lower bound of the error probability with a non-biased random source can be found in [53]. We will follow that proof, adapting it to our case where necessary.

3.3 Schöning's random walk algorithm for the Boolean Satisfiability Problem

Assume that the input consists of a formula F that has only one satisfying assignment a_0, and that a_0 satisfies exactly one literal of each of the clauses of F. We will show below how such a formula can be approximated.

During each iteration of the algorithm, the Hamming distance between the current assignment a and a_0 either decreases by one (if the correct literal is guessed) or increases by one (if a wrong literal is guessed), with the exception that if a is the complement of a_0, the distance can only decrease by 1 and not increase. This can be modeled by a Markov chain M_1 with states $0, 1, \ldots, n$, where the number of each state corresponds to the number of bits in a that do not match the solution a_0. Let X_t describe the Hamming distance after the t-th iteration of the algorithm. Then we have transition probabilities

$$P(X_{t+1} = j-1 | X_t = j) = \frac{1}{k} - \delta \quad \text{and}$$
$$P(X_{t+1} = j+1 | X_t = j) = \frac{k-1}{k} + \delta \text{ for } 1 \leq j < n ,$$

with the special cases $P(X_{t+1} = 0 | X_t = 0) = 1$ and $P(X_{t+1} = n-1 | X_t = n) = 1$. We will be interested in the probabilites $P(\exists t \leq 3n : X_t = 0 | X_0 = j)$ for all $j \leq n$.

To make our analysis simpler, we will remove the reflecting end of the Markov chain and consider a new chain M_2 with infinitely many states $0, 1, \ldots$. Let Y_t be the state of this new Markov chain after step t, with transition probabilities

$$P(Y_{t+1} = j-1 | Y_t = j) = \frac{1}{k} - \delta \quad \text{and}$$
$$P(Y_{t+1} = j+1 | Y_t = j) = \frac{k-1}{k} + \delta \text{ for } j \geq 1 ,$$

with only one special case $P(Y_{t+1} = 0 | X_t = 0) = 1$. For $Y_0 = j$, the Markov chain reaches the state 0 if it moves j times into the direction of decreasing state number, plus one additional time for each step into the other direction. I.e., state 0 can be reached if i state-increasing and $i + j$ state-decreasing steps are performed. Let $q(i, j)$ be the probability that $Y_{2i+j} = 0$ and $Y_k > 0$ for $k < 2i + j$ (i.e. the Markov chain hits the state 0 for the first time in step $2i + j$).

Note that for M_1 the probability of reaching state 0 is actually higher than for M_2. However, both probabilities differ by at most a factor polynomial in n. This can be seen as follows:

3 Algorithms and non-perfect randomness

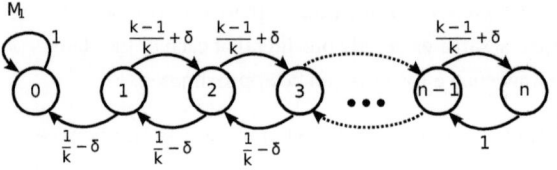

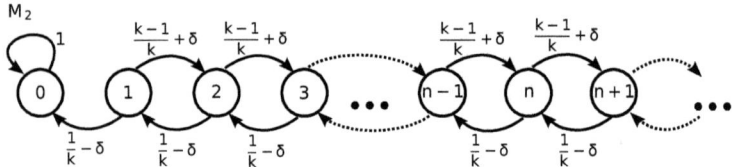

Figure 3.1: Two Markov chains describing the random process

Let $r_2(j,m)$ be the probability that Markov chain M_2 reaches the state 0 within m steps, starting in state j. Analogously, let $r_1(j,m)$ be the probability that M_1 reaches the state 0 within m steps, also starting in state j. Note that $\sum_{j=0}^{n} r_1(j,3n)$ describes the success probability of Algorithm 5, while we are going to analyse $\sum_{j=0}^{n} r_2(j,3n)$. Let $\hat{r}_1(j,m)$ be the probability that the Markov chain M_1 reaches state 0 after m steps, starting at state j, *without* visiting state n, and let $\tilde{r}_1(j,m,l)$ be the probability that M_1 visits state n exacly l times, returning to state j in step m, without visiting state j between the last visit of state n and step m. This way, $r_1(j,m)$ can be expressed as

$$r_1(j,m) = \hat{r}_1(j,m) + \sum_{l=1}^{3n} \sum_{k>1} \tilde{r}_1(j,k,l) \cdot \hat{r}_1(j,m-k) .$$

Since $\hat{r}_1(j,m-k) < \hat{r}_1(j,m)$ and $\sum_{k>1} \tilde{r}_1(j,k,l) < 1$ for all l, it holds that

$$\sum_{k>1} \tilde{r}_1(j,k,l) \hat{r}_1(j,m-k) < \hat{r}_1(j,m)$$

and thus

$$r_1(j,m) < (3n+1)\hat{r}_1(j,m) .$$

In the same way, we can define $\hat{r}_2(j,m)$ as the probability that M_2 reaches state 0 after m steps, starting at state j *without* visiting state n. Both Markov

3.3 Schöning's random walk algorithm for the Boolean Satisfiability Problem

chains show the same behavior as long as they do not touch state n, so clearly $\hat{r}_1(j,m) = \hat{r}_2(j,m)$, and we can derive

$$r_1(j,m) < (3n+1)\hat{r}_2(j,m) \leq (3n+1)r_2(j,m) \ .$$

This shows that the probabilities of the two Markov chains for reaching state 0 within $3n$ steps are equal up to a polynomial factor.

Now we analyze the probability $P(\exists t \leq 3n : Y_t = 0)$. Let $q(i,j)$ be the probability, that the Markov chain reaches state 0 in step $2i+j$ without reaching it before that step and under the condition that the chain starts in state j. This leads to

$$q(i,j) = \binom{2i+j}{i} \cdot \frac{j}{2i+j} \cdot \left(\frac{k-1}{k}+\delta\right)^i \cdot \left(\frac{1}{k}-\delta\right)^{i+j} \ .$$

Further define the probability that M_2 starts in state j as $p_j := P(Y_0 = j)$. Then we have

$$
\begin{aligned}
P(\exists t \leq 3n : Y_t = 0) &= \sum_{j=0}^{n} p_j \sum_{2i+j \leq 3n} q(i,j) \\
&= \sum_{j=0}^{n} p_j \sum_{i=0}^{(3n-j)/2} q(i,j) \\
&= \sum_{j=0}^{n} p_j \sum_{i=0}^{(3n-j)/2} \binom{2i+j}{i} \cdot \frac{j}{2i+j} \cdot \left(\frac{k-1}{k}+\delta\right)^i \cdot \left(\frac{1}{k}-\delta\right)^{i+j} \\
&\asymp \sum_{j=0}^{n} p_j \sum_{i=0}^{(3n-j)/2} \binom{2i+j}{i} \cdot \left(\frac{k-1}{k}+\delta\right)^i \cdot \left(\frac{1}{k}-\delta\right)^{i+j} \ .
\end{aligned}
$$

We now set $i = \alpha j$ and use the inequality

$$\binom{n}{\alpha n} \asymp \left(\left(\frac{1}{\alpha}\right)^\alpha \cdot \left(\frac{1}{1-\alpha}\right)^{1-\alpha}\right)^n$$

(which follows from Stirling's inequality, cf. [53]) to estimate

$$\sum_{j=0}^{n} p_j \sum_{i=0}^{(3n-j)/2} \binom{2i+j}{i} \cdot \left(\frac{k-1}{k}+\delta\right)^i \cdot \left(\frac{1}{k}-\delta\right)^{i+j}$$

3 Algorithms and non-perfect randomness

$$\asymp \sum_{j=0}^{n} p_j \sum_{i=0}^{(3n-j)/2} \left(\left(\frac{1+2\alpha}{\alpha}\right)^{\alpha} \cdot \left(\frac{1+2\alpha}{1+\alpha}\right)^{1+\alpha} \cdot \left(\frac{k-1}{k}+\delta\right)^{\alpha} \cdot \left(\frac{1}{k}-\delta\right)^{1+\alpha} \right)^{j}$$

$$\asymp \sum_{j=0}^{n} p_j \left(\frac{1-\delta k}{k-1+\delta k}\right)^{j}.$$

For the last asymptotic equality, we use the fact that the inner sum consists of only polynomially many summands and thus can be approximated (up to a polynomial factor) by its greatest summand. Setting the first derivative of that summand to zero results in $\alpha = \frac{1-\delta k}{k-2+2\delta k}$. Substituting that value into the summand leads to $\frac{1-\delta k}{k-1+\delta k}$. Assuming a uniform disitribution among all initial assignments, this leads to an asymptotic success probability of at most

$$2^{-n} \sum_{j=0}^{n} \binom{n}{j} \left(\frac{1-\delta k}{k-1+\delta k}\right)^{j} = 2^{-n} \left(1+\frac{1-\delta k}{k-1+\delta k}\right)^{n}$$

$$= \left(\frac{k}{2(k-1+\delta k)}\right)^{n}.$$

Using a random source with bias ε to construct the initial assignment a, we obtain a success probability of at most

$$\sum_{j=0}^{n} \binom{n}{j} \left(\frac{1}{2}-\varepsilon\right)^{j} \left(\frac{1}{2}+\varepsilon\right)^{n-j} \left(\frac{1-\delta k}{k-1+\delta k}\right)^{j}$$

$$= \left(\frac{1}{2}+\varepsilon+\left(\frac{1}{2}-\varepsilon\right)\left(\frac{1-\delta k}{k-1+\delta k}\right)\right)^{n}$$

$$= \left(\frac{k-2\varepsilon(k-2+2\delta k)}{2k-2+2\delta k}\right)^{n}.$$

We will now show how a worst case formula F can be approximated. We will demonstrate it for a 3-SAT formula, but this approach can be easily adapted to the case of larger k. First, fix a satisfying assignment $a_0 = (1,1,\ldots,1)$. Now define clauses

$$C_{i,j,k} := \{x_i, \neg x_j, \neg x_k\} \text{ for } 1 \leq i,j,k \leq n.$$

Additionally, define the four clauses

$$C'_0 := \{x_1, x_2, x_3\}, C'_1 := \{\neg x_1, x_2, x_3\}, C'_2 := \{x_1, \neg x_2, x_3\} \text{ and } C'_3 := \{x_1, x_2, \neg x_3\}.$$

3.3 Schöning's random walk algorithm for the Boolean Satisfiability Problem

At last, define the formula

$$F = \bigcup_{1 \leq i,j,k \leq n} C_{i,j,k} \cup \{C'_0, C'_1, C'_2, C'_3\} \ .$$

This formula has only one satisfying assignment: C'_0, C'_1, C'_2 and C'_3, along with $C_{1,2,3}, C_{2,1,3}$ and $C_{3,1,2}$, ascertain that the variables x_1, x_2 and x_3 have to be set to 1. Then, for any $i \in \{4, 5, \ldots, n\}$, $C_{i,1,2}$ forces x_i to be set to 1, too. Additionally, as long as a_0 has not been found and at least two variables are set to 1, the algorithm will choose a null-clause of the form $C_{i,j,k}$ (Remember that we assume that the first null-clause in the formula is chosen). Only in the case where only one variable is set to 1, the algorithm will choose one of the clauses C'_0, C'_1, C'_2 or C'_3 and have a higher probability to guess correctly. However, the success probability will not exceed that of an idealized formula as assumed in the proof, if we consider a formula with only $n-1$ variables. Thus, our formula will reach the proven success probability up to a polynomial factor. ∎

Note that for both random sources, it suffices that the random source has a constant bias towards one number. The worst-case formula can then be chosen corresponding to that bias. A "malign source" that can react to the algorithms random choices, like e.g. the δ-random source, is not necessary.

How a slight bias can mislead a probabilistic algorithm

Many probabilistic algorithms (e.g. the Miller-Rabin primality test) are based on a probabilistic algorithm with one sided error. It is a common approach to construct a new algorithm that repeats the original probabilistic algorithm $\Theta(1/p)$ times where p is the one-sided error probability of that algorithm. If all of these runs give the same result, the new algorithm gives that result, too. Otherwise, the new algorithm uses the result that can only be output when the original algorithm doesn't err. The new algorithm then runs successfully if at least one of the runs does not err. Repeating the algorithm $20/p$ times, for example, leads to an error probability $\tilde{p}$ of

$$\tilde{p} = (1-p)^{\frac{20}{p}} = \left((1-p)^{\frac{1}{p}}\right)^{20} \approx e^{-20} \ .$$

3 Algorithms and non-perfect randomness

In the case of the random walk SAT algorithm that has a (proven) success probability of $(3/4)^n$ for inputs with n variables, the algorithm has to be run $\Theta((4/3)^n)$ times in order to guarantee an error probability that is negligibly small.

Note however that a slight bias in the base error probability might strongly influence the algorithm's result. Assume that a single run of an algorithm with one-sided error has a small success probability of p^n. Repeating that algorithm $\frac{20}{p^n}$ times will decrease the error probability to

$$(1-p^n)^{\frac{20}{p^n}} \approx e^{-20} .$$

However, if the usage of a biased random source leads to a success probability of $(p-\varepsilon)^n$, repeating the algorithm $\frac{20}{p^n}$ times leads to an error probability of

$$(1-(p-\varepsilon)^n)^{\frac{20}{p^n}} = (1-(p-\varepsilon)^n)^{\frac{20(p-\varepsilon)^n}{p^n(p-\varepsilon)^n}}$$
$$\approx e^{-20\left(\frac{p-\varepsilon}{p}\right)^n} .$$

For any $\varepsilon > 0$, this new error probability limits to 1 for $n \to \infty$. In the case of the random walk SAT algorithm, this will lead to wrong results if n is large enough.

3.3 Schöning's random walk algorithm for the Boolean Satisfiability Problem

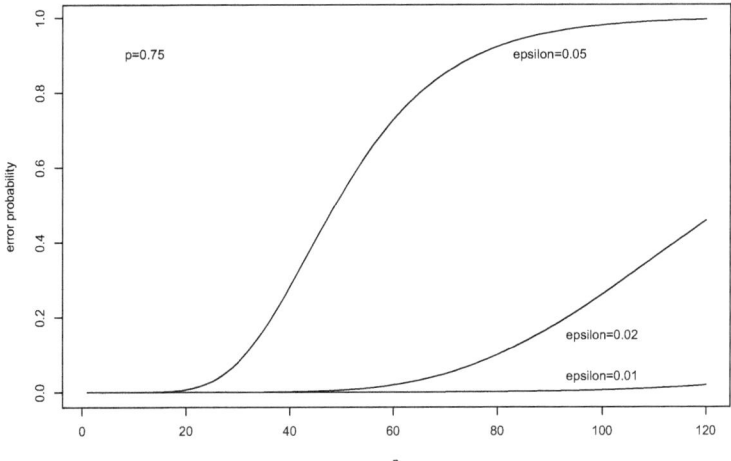

Figure 3.2: Overall error of a randomized algorithm after repeating. Assumed success probability of a single run is $\left(\frac{3}{4}\right)^n$, thus the algorithm is repeated $20 \cdot \left(\frac{4}{3}\right)^n$ times. Actual error probability of $\left(\frac{3}{4} - \varepsilon\right)^n$. Plot shown for three values of ε.

3 Algorithms and non-perfect randomness

4 Randomized QuickSort

Sorting is one of the most common and basic tasks in computer science. Sorting is used by database systems, greedy strategies, population based search heuristics, geometric algorithms (e.g. sweep line algorithms) and many more.

Every sorting algorithm which is based on pairwise comparisons of elements has to identify, from an information theoretic point of view, which of the $n!$ many input permutations is actually present (and using this information, the algorithm has to rearrange the elements physically to form a sorted sequence). Each comparison of two elements gives the algorithm one bit of information. Therefore, for the entire sorting process the algorithm needs, in the worst case, at least $\log_2(n!) = n\log_2 n - \Theta(n)$ many bits of information, or comparisons. Here we assume that each permutation of the input has the same probability. However, if there is no uniform distribution on the input set, then that lower bound decreases to $H(\mathcal{P})$, the entropy of the distribution $\mathcal{P}$ on the $n!$ possible input permutations.

This consideration can also be generalized to sorting methods that are not based on pairwise comparisons, like BucketSort: These methods can aquire more than 1 bit of information per "comparison", but still have to gain a total of $H(\mathcal{P})$ bits. BucketSort with k buckets can collect at most $\log k$ bits per step (where we only count the calculation of the correct bucket as a "step"). That way, we can derive a lower bound for the running time of $\Omega\left(\frac{n \cdot \log n}{\log k}\right)$. Note that when using only $\sqrt{n}$ buckets, this bound is not tight, because the BucketSort algorithm can only map each element once to the corresponding bucket and thus collect only $n\log \sqrt{n}$ bits of information. Then still $\theta(n\log n)$ bits of information are missing that have to be collected via pairwise comparisons.

In this chapter, we will take a deeper look at the QuickSort algorithm. This algorithm has been invented by C.A.R. Hoare in the sixties [5]. Knuth [54, page

4 Randomized QuickSort

115] coins this paper as one of the most comprehensive accounts of a sorting method that has ever been published. Later, Hoare received the ACM Turing Award 1980, and he was knighted for his achievements in Computer Science by Queen Elizabeth II in 2000.

QuickSort is a classical divide and conquer method: the input sequence is divided into two subsequences which are both sorted by applying the QuickSort algorithm recursively. Then these sorted sequences are concatenated together to form the desired sorted sequence. Unlike other divide and conquer algorithms, the input sequence is not necessarily split into two parts of equal sizes. Actually the sizes depend on the input itself. In each recursive step, a splitting element (the "pivot") is selected, which, in many implementations, is the first element of the sequence to be sorted. The sizes of the subsequences depend on the rank of the pivot element within the sequence to be sorted (which is not known beforehand).

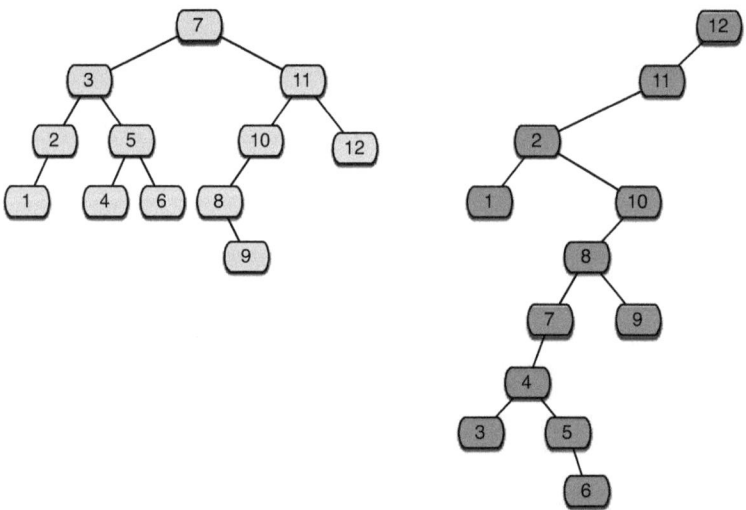

Figure 4.1: Two different recursion trees for RandomizedQuickSort. The numbers at the vertices denote the chosen pivot element. The sum of the vertex depths (distances to the root) corresponds to the number of comparisons. Left tree: 25 comparisons. Right tree: 51 comparisons.

It is known that QuickSort's average number of pairwise element comparisons (averaging over all potential input permutations) is $(2\ln 2)\cdot n\log_2 n - \Theta(n)$, so it is quite close to the ideal case, the lower bound. On the other hand, there are worst case inputs where QuickSort does up to $n(n-1)/2$ comparisons (ironically, the already sorted sequence has this property.) Realizing this bad worst-case behavior, Hoare already suggested the variant called Random QuickSort. In Random QuickSort (see Figure 4) the pivot element is selected uniformly at random among the elements of the sequence to be sorted. A very similar analysis as the one mentioned above shows that the expected number of comparisons, *for each input sequence*, is $(2\ln 2)\cdot n\log_2 n - \Theta(n)$. Here the expectation is taken over all random choices done in the course of the algorithm.

input: finite sequence $A = (a[1],a[2],\ldots a[n])$ of distinct elements
output: finite sequence B that contains all elements from A in increasing order
method: if A contains at most 1 element
      return A
  else
      Choose a random element x from A
      Split A into two subsequences A_1 and A_2 such that
        a) A_1 contains all elements from A smaller than x
        b) A_2 contains all elements from A greater than x
      $B_1 \leftarrow$ **QuickSort**(A_1)
      $B_2 \leftarrow$ **QuickSort**(A_2)
      return $B_1 \circ (x) \circ B_2$ ($\circ$ denotes concatenation)

Figure 4.2: Pseudo code of the randomized QuickSort algorithm

This analysis uses, as already mentioned, ideal random numbers, i.e. those being independent and uniformly distributed. Technically, such random numbers are difficult to produce, and in practice, one uses pseudorandom number generators instead, which start with some given "seed" x_0, and iteratively (and deterministically) compute successive values $x_{i+1} = f(x_i)$ according to some function f such that the obtained sequence of values $x_1, x_2, \ldots$ "looks random" (i.e. it passes some statistical tests). If the seed is fixed in advance, then the entire algorithm becomes a deterministic algorithm, and actually the above assertion about the existence of worst-case inputs with $n(n-1)/2$ many comparisons is still valid.

4 Randomized QuickSort

From a theoretical point of view, one might consider the seed of the pseudorandom generator as truly random. But still, under this theoretical model, when using a linear congruential generator, like $x_{i+1} = (ax_i + b) \mod c$ as suggested by D.H. Lehmer [44], Karloff and Raghavan [50] (see also [55]) have shown (under mild assumptions about the choice of the parameters a, b, c) that the expected number of comparisons can be, in the worst case, up to dn^2, for some constant d. Here the expectation is taken over the random choice of the seed, and the worst-case refers to the choice of the input.

In this chapter we follow this line of research and consider a random number generator for Random QuickSort which is not ideal. We measure the deficiency of the random number generator in terms of C.E. Shannon's entropy function $H(p_1, \ldots, p_n) = -\sum_{i=1}^{n} p_i \log p_i$ (see [3]). Depending on the Shannon entropy of the random number generator we show a continous transition between the "ideal" case of a $(n \log n)$-behavior and the "bad" case of (n^2)-behavior.

Recursion for the expected number of comparisons

Let $T_\pi(n)$ be the expected number of comparisons done by randomized QuickSort when operating on an input array $(a[1], \ldots, a[n])$ whose elements are distinct and permuted according to $\pi \in S_n$, that is,

$$a[\pi(1)] < a[\pi(2)] < \ldots < a[\pi(n)]$$

where S_n is the set of all permutations on $\{1, \ldots, n\}$.

Let X be a random variable taking values between 1 and n (not necessarily under uniform distribution) which models the random number generator that is used to pick out a pivot element $a[X]$. We say an element has rank i within the ordering of the array if there are exactly $i - 1$ smaller elements in the array. Let p_i be the probability that the pivot element has rank i within the ordering of the array, that is, $p_i = Pr(\pi(X) = i)$.

We obtain the following recursion for the expected worst case complexity (i.e. number of comparisons) $T(n) = \max_{\pi \in S_n} T_\pi(n)$. We have $T(n) = 0$ for $n \leq 1$; and for $n > 1$ we get

$$\begin{aligned}
T(n) &= \max_{\pi \in S_n} T_\pi(n) \\
&= (n-1) + \max_{\pi \in S_n} \sum_{i=1}^{n} p_i(T_\pi(i-1) + T_\pi(n-i)) \\
&\leq (n-1) + \sum_{i=1}^{n} p_i \left(\max_{\phi \in S_{i-1}} T_\phi(i-1) + \max_{\psi \in S_{n-i}} T_\psi(n-i) \right) \\
&= (n-1) + \sum_{i=1}^{n} p_i(T(i-1) + T(n-i)) \ .
\end{aligned}$$

That is, there are $n-1$ comparisons with the selected pivot element, and depending on the rank i of the pivot element within the array, there are at most $T_\pi(i-1)$ and $T_\pi(n-i)$ additional comparisons. If the rank of the pivot element is not uniformly distributed among the numbers 1 to n, a worst case input permutation can be constructed such that the middle ranks receive relatively low probability and the extreme ranks (close to 1 or close to n) get relatively high probability, resulting in a large expected number of comparisons.

We give upper and lower bounds on the expected number $T(n)$ of comparisons. Lower bounds are given with respect to a fixed worst case input sequence (e.g. the already sorted list of elements). These bounds are tight up to a logarithmic factor.

We can show (see Theorem 4.1) that $T(n) \leq g(n) n \log_2 n$ for any function $g(n)$ greater than $1/(\min_\pi \sum_{i=1}^{n} p_i H(i/n))$, where H is Shannon's binary entropy function. Note that $\min_\pi \sum_{i=1}^{n} p_i H(i/n)$ is independent of the permutation of the elements, i.e. is identical for all distributions p and q such that $p_i = q_{\pi(i)}$ for all i and some permutation π.

The lower bound (see Theorem 4.2) is derived for distributions on the ranks of the input elements. Therefore the lower bound $T(n) \geq cng(n)$ (Theorem 4.2) is with respect to any function $g(n)$ less than $1/\sum_{i=1}^{n} p_i H(i/(n+1))$, where p_i is the probability of selecting the element of rank i within the input a as a pivot element.

4 Randomized QuickSort

4.1 An upper bound

Let $(P_1, P_2, \ldots)$ denote a sequence of probability distributions with the property that $P_n = (p_{n1}, \ldots, p_{nn})$ is a distribution on $\{1, \ldots, n\}$.

Theorem 4.1 (cf. [14]) *Let $(P_1, P_2, \ldots)$ be a sequence of probability distributions on the indexes of the pivot elements used by Randomized QuickSort. Then the expected number of comparisons $T(n) \leq g(n) n \log_2 n$ for any monotone increasing function g with the property*

$$g(n) \geq \left(\min_{\pi \in S_n} \sum_{i=1}^n p_{n\pi^{-1}(i)} \cdot H\left(\frac{i}{n}\right) \right)^{-1}$$

where $H(x) = -x \log_2 x - (1-x) \log_2 (1-x)$ is Shannon's binary entropy function.

Proof. By induction on n. Using the above recursion for $T(n)$ we obtain

$$T(n) = (n-1) + \max_{\pi \in S_n} \sum_{i=1}^n p_{n\pi^{-1}(i)} (T_\pi(i-1) + T_\pi(n-i))$$

$$\leq n + \max_{\pi \in S_n} \sum_{i=1}^n p_{n\pi^{-1}(i)} (g(i-1)(i-1) \log_2(i-1) + g(n-i)(n-i) \log_2(n-i))$$

$$\leq n + g(n) n \max_{\pi \in S_n} \sum_{i=1}^n p_{n\pi^{-1}(i)} \left(\frac{i}{n} \log_2 i + \left(1 - \frac{i}{n}\right) \log_2(n-i) \right)$$

$$= n + g(n) n \max_{\pi \in S_n} \sum_{i=1}^n p_{n\pi^{-1}(i)} \left(\frac{i}{n} \log_2 \frac{i}{n} + \left(1 - \frac{i}{n}\right) \log_2 \left(1 - \frac{i}{n}\right) + \log_2 n \right)$$

$$= n + g(n) n \log_2 n - g(n) n \min_{\pi \in S_n} \sum_{i=1}^n p_{n\pi^{-1}(i)} H\left(\frac{i}{n}\right).$$

To finish the induction proof, this last expression should be at most $g(n) n \log_2 n$. This holds if and only if $g(n) \geq \left(\min_{\pi \in S_n} \sum_{i=1}^n p_{n\pi^{-1}(i)} H\left(\frac{i}{n}\right) \right)^{-1}$ as claimed. ∎

Example 1: In the standard case of a uniform distribution $p_{ni} = \frac{1}{n}$ we obtain $g(n) \geq \left(\frac{1}{n} \sum_{i=1}^n H\left(\frac{i}{n}\right)\right)^{-1}$. Asymptotically, this is $\left(\int_0^1 H(x) dx\right)^{-1} = 2 \ln 2$, which is the known constant factor of QuickSort's average running time.

Example 2: In the median-of-three version of QuickSort (cf. [54, 56]), three different elements are picked uniformly at random and the median of the three is used as the pivot element. In this case $p_{ni} = \frac{6(i-1)(n-i)}{n(n-1)(n-2)}$. Here the constant factor of the $n \log n$-term can be asymptotically estimated by

$$\left(6 \int_0^1 x(1-x) H(x) dx \right)^{-1} = \frac{12 \ln 2}{7} \approx 1.18 \; .$$

This matches the average running time given in [56].

4.2 A lower bound

In a similar fashion, we can derive a lower bound for the number of comparisons.

The running time derived in the upper bound theorem was independent of the actual input permutation and depended only on the distributions on the indices that are used to pick a pivot element from the input. Our lower bound however can not be that flexible: For every distribution on the indices of the input, there exists an input that will be divided into two subarrays of approximately equal sizes with high probability. Therefore, the theorem for the lower bound is formulated with respect to distributions on the ranks of the input numbers. Similar to Theorem 4.1 we get:

Theorem 4.2 *Let $(P_1, P_2, \ldots)$ be a sequence of probability distributions on the ranks of the chosen pivot elements, where $P_n = (p_{n1}, \ldots, p_{nn})$ is used to choose a pivot element from sequences of length n and the element of rank i is chosen with probability p_{ni}.*
(i) $T(n) \geq cg(n)n - n$ for some constants $c > 0$ and n_0, if for all $n > n_0$, g satisfies the two conditions

$$g(n) \leq \left(\sum_{i=1}^n p_{ni} \left(1 - \frac{(i-1)^2}{n^2} - \frac{(n-i)^2}{n^2} \right) \right)^{-1} \quad \text{and}$$

$$\frac{g(i)}{g(n)} \geq \frac{i}{n} \quad \text{for all} \quad 0 \leq i \leq n.$$

4 Randomized QuickSort

(ii) Part (i) still holds if we replace the two conditions by

$$g(n) \leq \left(\sum_{i=1}^{n} p_{ni} H\left(\frac{i}{n+1}\right)\right)^{-1} \quad \text{and}$$

$$\frac{g(i)}{g(n)} \geq \frac{i}{n} \quad \text{for all } 0 \leq i \leq n.$$

Proof. We prove (i) first, by induction. For $n \leq n_0$, just set the constant $c \leq 1$ small enough.

Now we look at the case $n > n_0$. Let $P_n = (p_{n1}, \ldots, p_{nn})$ be a distribution where p_{ni} is the probability that we choose as a pivot element the element with rank i. Using the induction hypothesis, it holds that

$$T(i-1) + T(n-i)$$
$$\geq c(i-1)g(i-1) + c(n-i)g(n-i) - (n-1)$$
$$= cng(n)\left(\frac{(i-1)g(i-1)}{ng(n)} + \frac{(n-i)g(n-i)}{ng(n)}\right) - (n-1)$$
$$\geq cng(n)\left(\frac{(i-1)^2}{n^2} + \frac{(n-i)^2}{n^2}\right) - (n-1)$$
$$= cng(n) - cng(n)\left(1 - \frac{(i-1)^2}{n^2} - \frac{(n-i)^2}{n^2}\right) - (n-1).$$

Therefore,

$$T(n) = n - 1 + \sum_{i=1}^{n} p_{ni}(T(i-1) + T(n-i))$$
$$\geq cng(n) - cng(n) \sum_{i=1}^{n} p_{ni}\left(1 - \frac{(i-1)^2}{n^2} - \frac{(n-i)^2}{n^2}\right).$$

As $c \leq 1$, we can finish the induction if

$$g(n) \leq \left(\sum_{i=1}^{n} p_{ni}\left(1 - \frac{(i-1)^2}{n^2} - \frac{(n-i)^2}{n^2}\right)\right)^{-1}.$$

The proof of part (ii) is quite similar: For $n \geq n_0$,

$$T(i-1) + T(n-i)$$

$$\geq cng(n)\left(\frac{(i-1)^2}{n^2}+\frac{(n-i)^2}{n^2}\right)-(n-1)$$

$$= cng(n)\left(\frac{(i-1)^2}{n^2}+\frac{(n-i)^2}{n^2}+H\left(\frac{i}{n+1}\right)\right)-ng(n)H\left(\frac{i}{n+1}\right)-(n-1)$$

$$\geq cng(n)-cng(n)H\left(\frac{i}{n+1}\right)-(n-1).$$

The last inequality uses Lemma 1.2. Now

$$T(n) = n-1+c\sum_{i=1}^{n}p_{ni}(T(i-1)+T(n-i))$$

$$\geq cng(n)-cng(n)\sum_{i=1}^{n}p_{ni}H\left(\frac{i}{n+1}\right).$$

Again using $c \leq 1$, we can finish the induction if

$$g(n) \leq \left(\sum_{i=1}^{n}p_{ni}H\left(\frac{i}{n+1}\right)\right)^{-1}.$$

Remark. In the second part of Theorem 4.2 the lower bound is given using the entropy function, similar to the upper bound in Theorem 4.1. This shows that up to a logarithmic factor we yield matching upper and lower bounds.

Note that the condition $g(i)/g(n) \geq i/n$ actually is not a limitation: We already know that QuickSort's running time ranges from $n\log_2 n$ to n^2, so our function g will meet the condition anyway.

4.3 Distributions with bounded entropy

The uniform distribution on $[1,n] = \{1,\ldots,n\}$ has maximal entropy. In this section we consider distributions which have bounded entropy.

4 Randomized QuickSort

Uniform distributions on subsets of $\{1,\ldots,n\}$

First we consider distributions with positive probability on subsets of $[1,n]$. Let $t(n) = o(n)$ be a monotone (increasing) function. Define a sequence of distributions $(P_1, P_2, \ldots)$ with $P_n = (p_{n1}, \ldots, p_{nn})$ such that

$$p_{ni} = \begin{cases} 1/t(n) & \text{if rank } a_i \leq t(n)/2 \text{ or rank } a_i > n - t(n)/2 \\ 0 & \text{otherwise} \end{cases}$$

That is, we choose the pivot element randomly using a uniform distribution among only the worst $t(n)$ array elements.

Now $\sum_{i=1}^{n} p_{ni} H(i/(n+1))$ resp. $\sum_{i=1}^{n} p_{ni} H(i/n)$ are bounded as follows:

$$\sum_{i=1}^{n} p_{ni} H\left(\frac{i}{n+1}\right) \leq \frac{t(n)}{2n} \log(n+1), \text{ and}$$

$$\sum_{i=1}^{n} p_{ni} H\left(\frac{i}{n}\right) \geq \frac{t(n)}{4n} \log\left(\frac{2n}{t(n)}\right).$$

This gives $T(n) \leq n \log(n) \frac{4n}{t(n)}$ as an upper bound and $T(n) \geq \frac{cn^2}{t(n) \log n} - n$ as a lower bound, for some constant c.

Proof. An upper bound $T(n) \leq g(n) n \log_2 n$ can be estimated as follows.

$$\begin{aligned}
\sum_{i=1}^{n} p_{ni} H\left(\frac{i}{n}\right) &= 2 \sum_{i=1}^{t(n)/2} \frac{1}{t(n)} H\left(\frac{i}{n}\right) = \frac{2}{t(n)} \sum_{i=1}^{t(n)/2} H\left(\frac{i}{n}\right) \\
&= \frac{2}{t(n)} \sum_{i=1}^{t(n)/2} -\left(\frac{i}{n} \log\left(\frac{i}{n}\right) + \frac{n-i}{n} \log\left(\frac{n-i}{n}\right)\right) \\
&\geq \frac{2}{t(n)} \sum_{i=1}^{t(n)/2} \frac{i}{n} \log\left(\frac{n}{i}\right) \geq \frac{2}{nt(n)} \log\left(\frac{2n}{t(n)}\right) \sum_{i=1}^{t(n)/2} i \\
&\geq \frac{2}{nt(n)} \log\left(\frac{2n}{t(n)}\right) \frac{(t(n)/2)(t(n)/2+1)}{2} \\
&\geq \frac{t(n)}{4n} \log\left(\frac{2n}{t(n)}\right).
\end{aligned}$$

With $g(n) = \frac{4n}{t(n) \log(2n/t(n))}$, it follows that $T(n) \leq \frac{4n^2}{t(n)} \frac{\log_2 n}{\log_2(2n/t(n))}$ (see Theorem 4.1).

4.3 Distributions with bounded entropy

In the same way the lower bound can be calculated:

$$\sum_{i=1}^{n} p_{ni} H\left(\frac{i}{n+1}\right)$$

$$= 2 \sum_{i=1}^{t(n)/2} \frac{1}{t(n)} H\left(\frac{i}{n+1}\right)$$

$$= \frac{2}{t(n)} \sum_{i=1}^{t(n)/2} \left(-\left(\frac{i}{n+1} \log\left(\frac{i}{n+1}\right) + \frac{n-i+1}{n+1} \log\left(\frac{n-i+1}{n+1}\right) \right) \right)$$

$$\leq \frac{2}{t(n)} \sum_{i=1}^{t(n)/2} 2 \frac{i}{n+1} \log\left(\frac{n+1}{i}\right)$$

$$= \frac{4}{(n+1)t(n)} \sum_{i=1}^{t(n)/2} i \log\left(\frac{n+1}{i}\right)$$

$$= \frac{4}{(n+1)t(n)} \left(\sum_{i=1}^{t(n)/2} i \log(n+1) - \sum_{i=1}^{t(n)/2} i \log i \right)$$

$$\leq \frac{4}{(n+1)t(n)} \left(\sum_{i=1}^{t(n)/2} i \log(n+1) - \int_{i=0}^{t(n)/2} x \log x \, dx \right)$$

$$= \frac{4 \log(n+1)}{(n+1)t(n)} \left(\frac{(t(n)/2)(t(n)/2+1)}{2} - \frac{1}{2}(t(n)/2)^2 \log(t(n)/2) + \frac{1}{4 \ln(2)} (t(n)/2)^2 \right)$$

$$= \frac{t(n) \log(n+1)}{n+1} \left(1 + \frac{1}{t(n)} - \frac{\log t(n)}{2} + \frac{1}{4 \ln(2)} \right)$$

$$\leq \frac{2.4 t(n) \log(n+1)}{n+1}$$

where we use that $t(n) \geq 1$.
With the function $g(n) = \frac{n+1}{2.4 t(n) \log(n+1)}$, we receive a lower bound of

$$T(n) \geq \frac{cn(n+1)}{t(n) \log(n+1)} - n = \Omega\left(\frac{n^2}{t(n) \log n} - n\right). \blacksquare$$

Min-Entropy

Uniform distributions on subsets of $[1,\ldots,n]$ are a special case of distributions with bounded *min-entropy*.

Definition 23 *A distribution* $(p_1,\ldots,p_n)$ *has min-entropy* k *if* $\max_i p_i = 2^{-k}$ *(cf.*

75

4 Randomized QuickSort

[23]).

Let $(P_1, P_2, \ldots)$ be a sequence of probability distributions such that every distribution $P_{nn} = (p_{n1}, \ldots, p_{nn})$ has min-entropy $k(n)$. Then we get an upper bound of $T(n) \leq \frac{4n^2}{2^{k(n)}}$ and a lower bound of $T(n) \geq \frac{cn^2}{2^{k(n)} \log n} - n$, for $c > 0$.

Proof. We have

$$\sum_{i=1}^n p_{ni} H(i/n) \geq 2 \sum_{i=1}^{2^{k(n)}/2} \frac{1}{2^{k(n)}} H(i/n)$$

$$\geq \frac{2^{k(n)}}{4n} \log\left(\frac{2n}{2^{k(n)}}\right) \text{, and}$$

$$\sum_{i=1}^n p_{ni} H\left(\frac{i}{n+1}\right) \leq 2 \sum_{i=1}^{2^{k(n)}/2} \frac{1}{2^{k(n)}} H\left(\frac{i}{n+1}\right)$$

$$\leq \frac{2^{k(n)}+1}{2(n+1)} \log\left(\frac{2(n+1)}{2^{k(n)}}\right)$$

and thus

$$T(n) \leq \frac{4n^2}{2^{k(n)}} \frac{\log_2 n}{\log_2(2n/2^{k(n)})}$$

and

$$T(n) \geq \frac{2cn(n+1)}{(2^{k(n)}+1)\log\left(\frac{2(n+1)}{2^{k(n)}}\right)} - n \ .$$

∎

So, for min-entropy 0 (this includes the deterministic case) we get

$$T(n) \leq \frac{4n^2}{1} \frac{\log_2 n}{\log_2(2n)} = 4n^2 \frac{\log_2 n}{\log_2 n + 1} \leq 4n^2 \quad \text{and}$$

$$T(n) \geq \frac{cn(n+1)}{\log(2(n+1))} - n \geq \frac{cn^2}{\log(n+1)+1} - n = \theta\left(\frac{n^2}{\log n}\right),$$

4.3 Distributions with bounded entropy

and for min-entropy $\log_2 n$ (all pivot elements are equally distributed), this leads to

$$T(n) \le \frac{4n^2 \log_2 n}{n \log_2 2} = 4n \log_2 n \ .$$

Bounds for geometric distributions

We consider the case that pivot elements are selected using a geometric distribution. The probability of picking an element with rank i as pivot is given by $p_i = q^{i-1}(1-q)$. More generally, we allow the geometric distribution to depend on the size n of the array, i.e., we define (P_i) using $q := 1 - \frac{1}{f(i)}$ for some (monotone) function $f = o(n)$. An additional probability of q^n is assigned to the best resp. worst pivot element (depending on if we consider a lower or upper bound), so that all p_i sum up to 1.

To estimate a lower bound on the number of comparisons, we use Theorem 4.2 and estimate $\sum_{i=1}^{n} p_{ni} \left(1 - \frac{(i-1)^2}{n^2} - \frac{(n-i)^2}{n^2}\right) \le \frac{cf(n)}{n}$, for a constant c.

Proof. Using the fact that $q^i = \left(1 - \frac{1}{f(n)}\right)^i = \left(1 - \frac{1}{f(n)}\right)^{f(n) \frac{i}{f(n)}} \le e^{-\frac{i}{f(n)}}$, it follows that

$$\sum_{i=1}^{n} p_{ni} \left(1 - \frac{(i-1)^2}{n^2} - \frac{(n-i)^2}{n^2}\right)$$

$$\le q^n \left(1 - \frac{(\frac{n}{2}-1)^2}{n^2} - \frac{(\frac{n}{2})^2}{n^2}\right) + \frac{1}{q} \sum_{i=1}^{n} q^i (1-q) \left(1 - \frac{(i-1)^2}{n^2} - \frac{(n-i)^2}{n^2}\right)$$

$$= q^n \left(\frac{1}{2} + \frac{1}{n} - \frac{1}{n^2}\right) + \frac{1}{qn^2} \sum_{i=1}^{n} q^i (1-q)(2ni + 2i - 2i^2 - 1)$$

$$\le q^n + \frac{1}{qn^2} \sum_{i=1}^{n} q^i (1-q)(2ni + 2i)$$

$$= \left(1 - \frac{1}{f(n)}\right)^n + \frac{2n+2}{\left(1 - \frac{1}{f(n)}\right) n^2} \sum_{i=1}^{n} \left(1 - \frac{1}{f(n)}\right)^i \frac{i}{f(n)}$$

$$= \left(1 - \frac{1}{f(n)}\right)^n + \frac{(2n+2)f(n)}{(f(n)-1)n^2} \sum_{i=1}^{n} \left(1 - \frac{1}{f(n)}\right)^i \frac{i}{f(n)} \ .$$

77

4 Randomized QuickSort

We split the sum and see that for $k = 0, 1, 2, \ldots$

$$\sum_{i=kf(n)+1}^{(k+1)f(n)} \left(1 - \frac{1}{f(n)}\right)^i \frac{i}{f(n)}$$

$$\leq \sum_{i=kf(n)+1}^{(k+1)f(n)} e^{-\frac{i}{f(n)} + \ln \frac{i}{f(n)}} = \sum_{j=1}^{f(n)} e^{-\frac{kf(n)+j}{f(n)} + \ln \frac{kf(n)+j}{f(n)}}$$

$$\leq \sum_{j=1}^{f(n)} e^{-k - \frac{j}{f(n)} + \ln(k+1)} = e^{-k + \ln(k+1)} \sum_{j=1}^{f(n)} e^{-\frac{j}{f(n)}}$$

$$\leq e^{-k + \ln(k+1)} f(n) \ .$$

Then we get

$$\left(1 - \frac{1}{f(n)}\right)^n + \frac{(2n+2)f(n)}{n^2(f(n)-1)} \sum_{i=1}^{n} \left(1 - \frac{1}{f(n)}\right)^i \frac{i}{f(n)}$$

$$= \left(1 - \frac{1}{f(n)}\right)^n + \frac{(2n+2)f(n)}{n^2(f(n)-1)} \sum_{k=0}^{\lceil n/f(n)\rceil} \sum_{i=kf(n)+1}^{(k+1)f(n)} \left(1 + \frac{1}{f(n)}\right)^i \frac{i}{f(n)}$$

$$\leq e^{-\frac{n}{f(n)}} + \frac{(2n+2)f(n)}{n^2(f(n)-1)} \sum_{k=0}^{\lceil n/f(n)\rceil} e^{-k + \ln(k+1)} f(n)$$

$$\leq e^{-\frac{n}{f(n)}} + \frac{(2n+2)f(n)^2}{n^2(f(n)-1)} \sum_{k=0}^{\infty} \frac{k+1}{e^k}$$

$$\leq \frac{cf(n)}{n} \text{ for a constant } c.$$

For the last inequality, note that $f(n) = o(n)$, so that $e^{-\frac{n}{f(n)}} = o\left(\frac{f(n)}{n}\right)$.

Using Theorem 4.2, we get a lower bound of $c'n^2/f(n)$ for the running time of the QuickSort algorithm, for some constant c'. ∎

To get an upper bound for geometric distributions we estimate similarly

$$\sum_{i=1}^{n} p_{ni} H\left(\frac{i}{n}\right) \geq \frac{f(n)}{n} \left(1 - e^{-\frac{n}{2f(n)}} \frac{n}{f(n)}\right) ,$$

which gives $T(n) \leq \frac{cn^2 \log n}{f(n)}$ as upper bound, for some $c > 0$.

4.3 Distributions with bounded entropy

Proof.

$$\sum_{i=1}^{n} p_{ni} H\left(\frac{i}{n}\right) = \frac{1-q}{q} \sum_{i=1}^{n} q^i H\left(\frac{i}{n}\right)$$

$$\geq \frac{1-q}{q} \sum_{i=1}^{n} q^i \left(\frac{i}{n} \log \frac{n}{i} + \frac{n-i}{n} \log \frac{n}{n-i}\right)$$

$$\geq \frac{1-q}{q} \sum_{i=1}^{n} q^i \left(\frac{i}{n} \log \frac{n}{i}\right)$$

$$\geq \frac{1-q}{qn} \log n \sum_{i=1}^{n-1} q^i i$$

$$= \frac{1-q}{qn} \log n \left(\frac{q^n(nq-n-q)}{(1-q)^2} + \frac{q}{(1-q)^2}\right)$$

$$= \frac{\log n}{n} \left(\frac{q^{n-1}(nq-n-q)}{1-q} + \frac{1}{1-q}\right)$$

We again set $q := 1 - \frac{1}{f(n)}$ to obtain

$$\sum_{i=1}^{n} p_{ni} H\left(\frac{i}{n}\right) = \frac{\log n}{n} \left(\frac{\left(1-\frac{1}{f(n)}\right)^{n-1}\left(n\left(1-\frac{1}{f(n)}\right)-n-1+\frac{1}{f(n)}\right)}{\frac{1}{f(n)}} + \frac{1}{\frac{1}{f(n)}}\right)$$

$$= \frac{\log n f(n)}{n} \left((n-1)\left(1-\frac{1}{f(n)}\right)^n - n\left(1-\frac{1}{f(n)}\right)^{n-1} + 1\right)$$

$$= \frac{\log n f(n)}{n} \left(\left(1-\frac{1}{f(n)}\right)^{n-1}\left((n-1)\left(1-\frac{1}{f(n)}\right)-n\right)+1\right)$$

$$= \frac{\log n f(n)}{n} \left(\left(1-\frac{1}{f(n)}\right)^{n-1}\left(-1-\frac{n-1}{f(n)}\right)+1\right)$$

$$= \frac{\log n f(n)}{n} \left(1-\left(1-\frac{1}{f(n)}\right)^{n-1}\left(1+\frac{n-1}{f(n)}\right)\right)$$

$$\geq \frac{\log n f(n)}{n} \left(1-e^{-\frac{n-1}{f(n)}}\frac{2n}{f(n)}\right)$$

$$\geq \frac{c \log n f(n)}{n} \quad \text{for some constant } c > 0 \text{ if } f(n) = o(n)$$

So we have an upper bound for the worst-case running time of $T(n) \leq \frac{cn^2}{f(n)}$ for

4 Randomized QuickSort

some constant $c > 0$.

4.4 Randomness as a resource for the QuickSort algorithm

When examining the performance of sorting algorithms, we usually measure their performance by counting the number of (pair-wise) comparisons that are needed to sort an input sequence. For randomized algorithms, we can also measure the number of random bits the algorithm requests to find a solution. The expected amount of random bits $H(n)$ needed by a run of QuickSort on n numbers can be expressed by the recurrence

$$\begin{aligned} H(n) &= \log_2 n + \frac{1}{n} \sum_{i=1}^{n} H(i-1) + H(n-i) \\ &= \log_2 n + \frac{2}{n} \sum_{i=0}^{n-1} H(i) \end{aligned}$$

This way we get

$$nH(n) - (n-1)H(n-1) = n\log_2 n - (n-1)\log_2(n-1) + 2H(n-1)$$

and

$$\frac{H(n)}{n+1} = \frac{H(n-1)}{n} + \frac{n\log_2 n - (n-1)\log_2(n-1)}{n(n+1)}.$$

Substituting $A(n) := \frac{H(n)}{n+1}$ results in

$$A(n) = A(n-1) + \frac{n\log_2 n - (n-1)\log_2(n-1)}{n(n+1)}$$

and thus

$$A(n) = \sum_{i=1}^{n} \frac{i\log_2 i - (i-1)\log_2(i-1)}{i(i+1)} \quad \text{and}$$

$$H(n) = (n+1) \sum_{i=1}^{n} \frac{i\log_2 i - (i-1)\log_2(i-1)}{i(i+1)}$$

4.4 Randomness as a resource for the QuickSort algorithm

$$= (n+1) \sum_{i=1}^{n} \frac{\log_2 i}{i(i+1)} \cdot \left(\frac{i \log_2 i - (i-1) \log_2(i-1)}{\log_2 i} \right) .$$

Using de l'Hôpital's rule twice, we see that

$$\lim_{i \to \infty} \frac{i \log_2 i - (i-1) \log_2(i-1)}{\log_2 i}$$

$$= \lim_{i \to \infty} \frac{\log_2 i - \log_2(i-1)}{\frac{1}{i}}$$

$$= \lim_{i \to \infty} \frac{\frac{1}{i \ln 2} - \frac{1}{(i-1) \ln 2}}{-\frac{1}{i^2}}$$

$$= \lim_{i \to \infty} \frac{i^2}{i(i-1) \ln 2} = \frac{1}{\ln 2} ,$$

and since $\sum_{i=1}^{n} \frac{\log_2 i}{i(i+1)} = \Theta(1)$, it follows that

$$H(n) = \Theta(n) .$$

This means that on the average a constant number of bits per input element is enough to guarantee an average case running time of $\Theta(n \log n)$.

Note: $H(n) = \Theta(n)$ can also be proven by induction. To do this, use the induction hypothesis $H(n) \leq cn - d \log_2 n$ for some constants c and d.

Note that the number of necessary random bits increases if the average running time of the algorithm increases, for example if these random bits are not uniformly distributed. In the case of the worst possible running time of $\Theta(n^2)$, the i-th pivot element has to be chosen out of a set of $n+1-i$ elements, so at least $\log_2(n+1-i)$ bits are needed. This leads to

$$H(n) = \sum_{i=1}^{n} \log_2 i$$

$$\geq \sum_{i=n/2}^{n} \log_2 \frac{n}{2} = \Theta(n \log n) .$$

So while the entropy of that sequence of "random" bits decreases (in the extreme

4 Randomized QuickSort

case, these bits don't have to be random any more), its length increases from $\Theta(n)$ in the optimal case to $\Theta(n \log n)$ in the deterministic case.

5 Local and population based search heuristics

In Chapters 3 and 4, we gave examples where we could show that the use of non-pefect random numbers can have an effect on the error probability resp. the run-time of a probabilistic algorithm. Similar results have been found by Karloff et al. [12] and Bach [13]. Generic probabilistic search heuristics like Simulated Annealing and Genetic Algorithms represent another interesting area of algorithms that use randomness in various ways. However, implications of using certain kinds of pseudorandom generators or other non-perfect sources of randomness have not yet been thoroughly examined. In the case of evolutionary algorithms, Meysenburg showed that a simple evolutionary algorithm's solution did not significally depend on the choice of the random number generator [15]. Tompkins and Hoos showed that stochastic local search methods for the satisfiability problem seem not to be influenced by the quality of the pseudorandom number generator [17].

We were interested in the effects of generators with very low quality on local search heuristics, especially Simulated Annealing, and population based heuristics like evolutionary algorithms. To this end, we conducted several experiments where we gradually decreased the quality of the pseudorandom number generators, and tested if this decrease in quality directly affected the output of the search heuristics.

5 Local and population based search heuristics

5.1 Search Heuristics

5.1.1 Simulated Annealing

The Simulated Annealing heuristic has been popularized by Kirkpatrick in 1983 [58] and is based on the Metropolis-Hastings algorithm [59] that dates back to 1953. Since then, it has been widely used for various optimization problems, e.g. the Traveling Salesman Problem. It simulates the cooling of physical matter, where a state changes to a state with higher energy only with a certain probability. This probability decreases during the proceeding of the algorithm. When optimizing a function f, we interpret $f(x)$ as the energy of state x. Beginning in a randomly chosen state, this state slightly changes step by step, i.e. transforms into a neighbor state. This transformation prefers new states with lower energy. The chance that the algorithm moves to a state of higher energy depends on a temperature parameter T, which is gradually decreased. When T decreases, the probability that a state transition with increasing energy is accepted decreases, too. This way, the system gradually tends to move towards lower energy states.

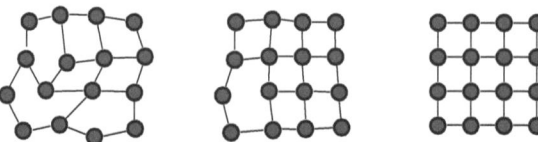

Figure 5.1: Sketch of the idea behind Simulated Annealing – Beginning in a state of high energy, that energy steadily decreases.

Simulated Annealing is a typical local search heuristic: Beginning at one point in the search space, the algorithm moves through the search space, in each step moving from one element to a neighbor of that element.

Pseudo code for Simulated Annealing is seen in Algorithm 6. For fixed temperature T, the algorithm simulates a Markov process where the variable x holds the random state. It was shown in [60] that this process limits to the Gibbs

Input: Function f
Output: x with f(x) as small as possible
Initialize temperature T;
$x \leftarrow$ random;
$m \leftarrow x$;
while $T > T_0$ **do**
    $y \leftarrow$ random neighbor of x;
    if $f(y) < f(x)$ **then**
        $x \leftarrow y$;
    else
        $x \leftarrow y$ with probability $e^{-\frac{f(y)-f(x)}{T}}$;
    end
    if $f(x) < f(m)$ **then**
        $m \leftarrow x$;
    end
    decrease T;
end
output m;

Algorithm 6: Pseudocode of the Simulated Annealing heuristic

distribution where an element x occurs with probability

$$P(x) = \frac{e^{-\frac{f(x)}{T}}}{\sum_x e^{-\frac{f(x)}{T}}}.$$

For $T \to \infty$, this distribution limits to the uniform distribution. For $T \to 0$, it limits to the uniform distribution on $\Omega_0 = \{x| \ f(x) = min_x f(x)\}$, the set of all global minima.

While for very low temperature T, the Markov chain converges to the set of solutions, it remains at *local* optima for many steps and only converges to the stationary distribution very slowly. To speed up convergence, Simulated Annealing starts with a high value of T and gradually lowers T. This random process does not have a stationary transition matrix like a Markov chain, but still converges to the uniform distribution on the global minima if $T(t) \to 0$ slowly enough. More precisely, let $T(t)$ be the temperature at iteration $t = 0, 1, 2, \ldots$ and let Ω_0 be the set of all global minima as defined above. Then the Simulated Annealing process converges to the uniform distribution on Ω_0 if $\lim_{t \to \infty} T(t) \to 0$

5 Local and population based search heuristics

and $T(t) \in \Omega(\frac{1}{\log n})$ (see [60]).

5.1.2 Population based heuristics

Population based search heuristics try to optimize a function by searching at many objects of the search space simultaneously. They are usually inspired by populations found in nature. Genetic algorithms, for example, are inspired by evolution. They are usually expressed in the form of a maximization problem, maximizing the "fitness", which is usually a non-negative function. An initial population changes during the course of time with the help of some basic operations:

- Selection: Each object of the population is evaluated with the help of a fitness function. Objects with a higher fitness are more likely to survive.
- Mutation: Some objects are slightly changed, for example by changing some bits of their binary representation.
- Crossover: Pairs of parent objects are combined into new objects that resemble both parent objects.

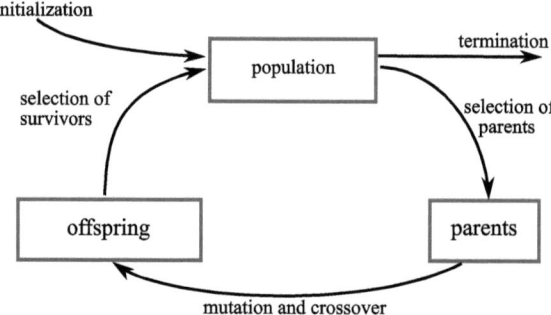

Figure 5.2: Sketch of a Genetic Algorithm.

Genetic algorithms use randomness at various places: The initial population is often chosen at random. The crossover and mutation operators are often applied to random objects, their probability usually depending on their individual fitness. When replacing unfit objects, we may choose these objects randomly,

5.1 Search Heuristics

too, for example by replacing objects with low fitness with high probability, but still allowing the replacement of individuals of higher fitness, with lower probability. This way, the population is kept diverse and is prevented from concentrating around a local optimum. For example, crossover with an unfit object might lead away from such a local optimum and help find the global optimum. The crossover itself might require random choices, too: This ranges from the choice of individuals that are combined to the concrete choice of which information is used from each of those individuals.

See Algorithm 7 for pseudocode of a basic genetic search heuristic.

Input: Function f
Output: x; the goal is to output an x with minimal $f(x)$.

Initialize population P;
repeat
    Replace unfit objects by mutations of fit objects;
    Replace unfit objects by crossover of fit objects;
until *termination condition* ;
Output best object found so far;

        Algorithm 7: Pseudocode for a simple evolutionary algorithm

If a random selection is desired, the roulette wheel algorithm is a good choice: It partitions the interval $[0,1)$ into subintervals such that there is a bijective mapping between the elements in the present generation and the subintervals. One element is then chosen by drawing a random uniformly distributed number in $[0,1)$ and identifying the unique subinterval and thus the corresponding element of the population. The sizes of the subintervals can be varied, e.g making their size proportional to the fitness value of their corresponding element or basing their size on the rank of the element among the population. The roulette wheel then selects every population element with probability equal to the size of the corresponding interval.

Listing 5.1 shows our concrete implementation of the roulette wheel (in the language *R*) used in the evolutionary algorithm. `fitt` is the vector of fitness values of all elements of the population, *number* is the number of indexes we want to select, and the argument `getNext` is a function that is used to create the pseudorandom numbers. roulette returns a vector of indexes, which we use to select objects from our population.

```
roulette <- function(fitt, number, getNext){
    fit         <- cumsum( fitt / sum(fitt) )
    selection <- double(number)

    for (i in 1:number){
        selection[i] <- which(fit >= getNext() )[1]
    }

    return(selection)
}
```

Listing 5.1: The roulette wheel

With the Schema Theorem, Holland formalized the evolution of a population's changes during the run of a genetic algorithm [61]. If each individual of a population is described by a binary string of length n, then a schema is a string of length n over the alphabet $\{0,1,*\}$. The $*$ is used as a wildcard: A schema represents all strings that are equal to the schema at all positions where the schema does not have a wildcard. The schema $110**1$, for example, represents all strings of length 6 that begin with 110 and end with 1. The fitness value $f(s)$ of a schema s is the average fitness value of all strings represented by s. The Schema Theorem considers the variant of a genetic algorithm shown as Algorithm 8.

Let $p(s,t)$ describe the proportion of strings represented by schema s in generation t, $f(s,t)$ the average fitness of all strings in the population represented by s at generation t, and $\overline{f}(t)$ the average fitness of the whole population at generation t. Assuming an infinite population, the Schema Theorem then bounds the proportion of s in generation $t+1$ by

$$p(s,t+1) \geq p(s,t) \left(\frac{f(s,t)}{\overline{f}(t)} \right) (1 - p_c p_d(s)(1 - p(s,t))) (1 - p_m(s)) ,$$

where p_c is the probability that an individual is "crossed over" with another individual, $p_d(s)$ is the probability that a crossover affects the positions specified in s, and $p_m(s)$ is the probability that mutation affects at least one position

5.1 Search Heuristics

Input: Non-negative fitness function f
Output: x; the goal is to output an x with maximal fitness $f(x)$.

Initialize population P of size M;
repeat
    $P' \leftarrow \emptyset$;
    repeat
        Choose an individual x from P with probability proportional to $f(x)$;
        With probability p_c,
            choose $y \in P$ under uniform distribution,
            $x \leftarrow$ crossover of x and y;
        Change each bit of x with probability p_m;
        Add x to P';
    until $|P'| = |P|$;
    Replace P by P'
until *termination condition* ;
Output best individual found so far;

Algorithm 8: Pseudocode of the genetic algorithm considered in the Schema Theorem

specified by s (see Algorithm 8). In the case of a finite population, replace $p(s,t+1)$ by its expected value $E(p(s,t+1))$.

Considering a finite population, the Schema Theorem describes how the presence of a schema representing good solutions grows, as soon as at least one individual is represented by that schema. As long as none of the individuals is represented by a given schema, one can only hope that the schema is introduced with the help of mutation or crossover. Note that the proportion of a schema in a finite population can even drop back to zero. Apart from that, a schema that represents the optimal solution, but contains many wildcards, does not necessarily have a good average fitness value; at the same time, a schema with good average fitness value does not necessarily represent the optimal solution. Therefore, the theorem only guarantees a fast convergence if *good solutions* share many bits with the *optimal solution*. In that case, however, one might be able to construct more specialized algorithms to solve the given problem.

5 Local and population based search heuristics

5.2 Implementation

Our experiments were implemented in *R* [29] and run on a system with *R* version 2.8.1 installed. We used *R* because it allows the quick development of code as well as an easy visualisation of the data. The *R* interface to the *C* language allowed us to implement the crossover operation for the evolutionary algorithm in *C*.

Listing 5.2 shows the basic implementation of a class rng, along with a subclass reference. The global object rng.reference is then created and a function reference.getNext defined, which gives us one random number each time we call it. The last output is stored in the global object, just in case we want to reuse it.

```
setClass("rng",
    representation(seed="numeric", range="numeric", state="numeric" )
);
setClass("reference",representation(),contains="rng")

rng.reference <- new("reference");

reference.getNext <- function() {
    rng.reference@state <<- runif(1,min=0,max=1);
    return(rng.reference@state);
}
```

Listing 5.2: The reference RNG, which uses R's builtin Mersenne Twister

One aspect of "quality" of a pseudorandom generator is its period length. In order to achieve pseudorandom sequences with scalable period length, we artificially shortened period lengths of PRNGs like the Mersenne Twister or Marsaglia's CD-ROM sequence by counting the output numbers and resetting the seed after a fixed amount of output numbers. On the one hand, this method enabled us to compare various pseudorandom sequences with equal period lengths. On the other hand, it allowed us to scale the period length of pseudorandom sequences that had otherwise a very long period length. Corresponding *R* code can be found in Listing 5.3. We simply count the number of output numbers and reset the seed when the output has reached a given length.

5.2 Implementation

```
setClass("mrepeater",representation(len="numeric"),contains="rng");

rng.mrepeater <- new("mrepeater");

mrepeater.getNext <- function() {
  rng.mrepeater@state <<- (rng.mrepeater@state%%rng.mrepeater@len)+1;
  if(rng.mrepeater@state == 1)
    set.seed(rng.mrepeater@seed);
  return(runif(1));
}
```

Listing 5.3: A Mersenne Repeater.

Our implementation of Simulated Annealing used a simplification to the original version: Instead of decreasing the temperature T after each run of the main loop, we only ran the algorithm for 100 different temperature values. For each of these values, the main loop was executed several times. For the Traveling Salesman Problem, for example, the procedure of creating a neighbor state and accepting resp. rejecting it was iterated 10,000 times for each temperature value. This method was used to prevent numerical problems that can arise when using factors close to 1. It allowed us to decrease the temperature by a factor of 0.97 after every 10,000 iterations instead of decreasing it by a factor of $\sqrt[10000]{0.97}$ after each iteration. To find a neighbor of a TSP tour, we switched two vertices of a tour, chosen at random. For example, the tour $(\ldots,x_{i-1},x_i,x_{i+1},\ldots,x_{j-1},x_j,x_{j+1},\ldots)$ is considered a neighbor of the tour $(\ldots,x_{i-1},x_j,x_{i+1},\ldots,x_{j-1},x_i,x_{j+1},\ldots)$. For DeJong's test functions, neighbors of a vector $(x_1,\ldots,x_n)$ were found by adding a random value to each component, drawn from a normal distribution with mean 0 and standard deviation equal to 0.02 times the size of the function's domain.

In the Genetic Algorithm, the mutation of an individual was implemented exactly the same way as finding a neighbor in Simulated Annealing. In the mutation step, we replaced 50% of the population. The selection step chose individuals for the next generation with the help of the roulette wheel algorithm described above. Crossover for the Traveling Salesman Problem was implemented as the edge-3 operator presented in [62]. Crossover for DeJong's test functions was implemented as follows: For two parents $x_1,\ldots,x_n$ and $y_1,\ldots,y_n$,

5 Local and population based search heuristics

a child $z_1,\ldots,z_n$ was constructed at random such that $P(z_i = x_i) = P(z_i = y_i) = 0.5$ (assuming a perfect source of randomness). In each loop, we checked that the best object so far was not removed from the population. In the crossover step, we replaced about 10% of the population by crossover offsprings. The algorithm terminated after a fixed number of loops.

5.3 Experimental Setup and Results

In our experiments, we were interested in the dependency between the quality of the pseudorandom generator and the quality of the solution given by two search heuristics, namely Simulated Annealing and an evolutionary algorithm.

One problem we used for our analysis was the Traveling Salesman Problem (short TSP).

Definition 24 *The* Traveling Salesman Problem *is defined as follows:*
Given a quadratic $n \times n$ matrix D of positive values (a distance matrix), what is the permutation $\pi \in S_n$ where

$$D_{\pi_n \pi_1} + \sum_{i=1}^{n-1} D_{\pi_i \pi_{i+1}}$$

is minimized?

Intuitively, The Traveling Salesman Problem asks for a tour that visits each of n nodes exactly once, then goes back to the initial node and minimizes the total cost of the tour. Costs for moving from any node i to a node j are given by the matrix entry D_{ij}, and to obtain the total cost of a tour, we can just add up the costs of the individual steps. The Traveling Salesman Problem is especially suited for our experiments because on the one hand, it is known that Simulated Annealing as well as Genetic Algorithms can be used to solve the Traveling Salesman Problem (see [63]), and on the other hand it is NP-complete, which ensures that our heuristics have to run for a rather long time in order to find a good solution.

5.3 Experimental Setup and Results

Another interesting set of test functions was published by DeJong [64] in 1975. The set was specfically designed to measure the performance of search heuristics and consists of the following 5 test functions:

- $f_1(x_1,\ldots,x_k) = \sum_{i=1}^{k} x_i^2$, with $-5.12 \leq x_i \leq 5.12$.

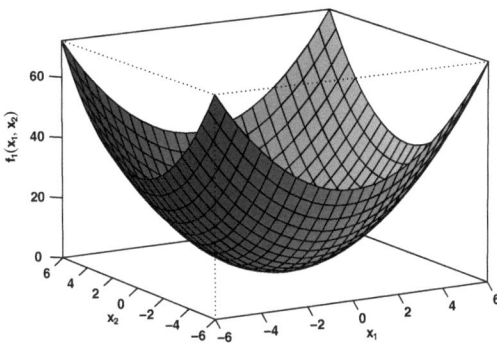

Figure 5.3: Plot of DeJong's function f_1.

This function should not be a problem for an optimization algorithm. The function is very smooth and has only one local minimum, which is also the global minimum. In DeJong's original publication [64], this function used $k = 2$. But in order to compare the effects of different pseudorandom sequences, we had to increase k and make the function more difficult to solve.

- $f_2(x_1,\ldots,x_k) = \sum_{i=1}^{k-1} \left(100(x_{i+1} - x_i^2)^2 + (x_i - 1)^2\right)^2$, with $-5.12 \leq x_i \leq 5.12$.

f_2 is more difficult to optimize: The minimum lies in a "valley" where function values only vary lightly, while outside of the valley the function values increase quickly.

- $f_3(x_1,\ldots,x_k) = 6k + \sum_{i=1}^{k} \lfloor x_i \rfloor$, with $-5.12 \leq x_i \leq 5.12$.

This function consists of many plateaus, where almost every point is a local minimum. Search algorithms with small step sizes could have problems optimizing this function, due to difficulties finding a good direction.

- $f_4(x_1,\ldots,x_k) = \sum_{i=1}^{k} i x_i^4 + \mathcal{N}(0,1)$, with $-5.12 \leq x_i \leq 5.12$.

f_4 is a polynomial function with additional noise. Each time the function is evaluated, a new term is added, drawn from a normal distribution with

5 Local and population based search heuristics

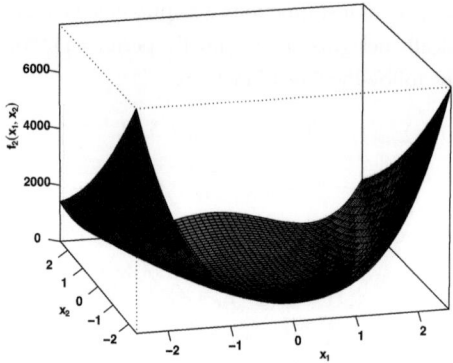

Figure 5.4: Partial plot of DeJong's function f_2. Only the central region is shown, without the steep slopes.

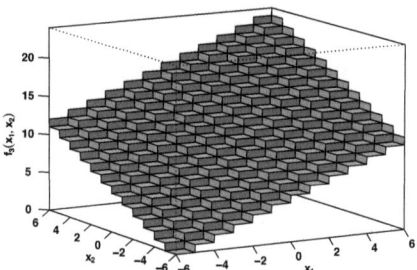

Figure 5.5: Plot of DeJong's function f_3.

mean 0 and variance 1. Some deterministic optimization methods, like the gradient descent method, have problems optimizing noisy functions.

- $f_5(x_1,x_2) = \left(0.002 + \sum_{j=1}^{25} \frac{1}{\sum_{i=1}^{2} j+(x_i-a_{ij})^6}\right)^{-1}$, with $-65.536 \leq x_i \leq 65.536$ and matrix
$$(a_{ij}) = \begin{pmatrix} -32 & -16 & 0 & 16 & 32 & \cdots & 0 & 16 & 32 \\ -32 & -32 & -32 & -32 & -32 & \cdots & 32 & 32 & 32 \end{pmatrix}.$$

This function has 25 local minima, with the global minimum near the point $(-32,-32)$. It was designed to "trap" optimization algorithms in one local optimum to research if they could still find a global optimum after finding a local one.

5.3 Experimental Setup and Results

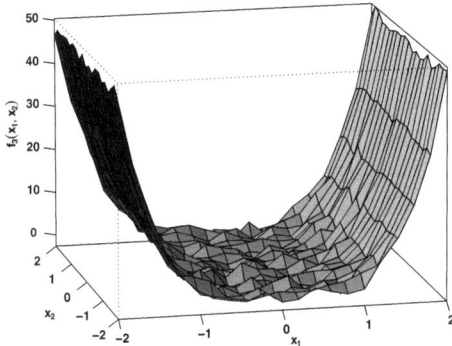

Figure 5.6: Schematic plot of DeJong's function f_4. Note that each time the function is evaluated, a new error term is added.

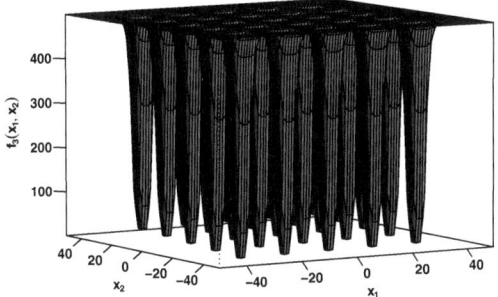

Figure 5.7: Plot of DeJong's function f_5.

Some of our experiments involve sequences of varying period lengths. To see how these were constructed, see Listing 5.3. It shows how we artificially reduced the period length of long pseudorandom sequences.

For the experiments on the Traveling Salesman Problem, we created eight random distance matrices with 50 cities each. In each of these matrices, the distances were chosen uniformly from the set $\{1,\ldots,40\}$. The matrices were created with the help of 4 different sources of randomness: Two were created with a Mersenne Twister, two with the stream cipher Trivium, two with the Diehard sequence, and two with a sequence of random bits obtained from a quantum experiment. The latter sequence was provided by Prof. Zeilinger's

5 Local and population based search heuristics

group at the University of Vienna. We will call this sequence the *quantum generator*.

The experiments were designed as complete block designs: For the experiments on the Traveling Salesman Problem, each pseudorandom sequence we were interested in was combined with each of the eight input matrices, usually started with 50 different seeds. For the experiments on the test functions, each pseudorandom sequence was combined with each sequence.

Representative parts of our results will be shown in boxplot diagrams: The three horizontal lines of a box represent first quantile, median and third quantile. The ends of the whiskers represent minimum and maximum values, where a whisker's maximum length is 1.5 times the interquartile range (distance between first and third quartile). Any values outside of that range are considered outliers and plotted as individual points.

5.3.1 Simulated Annealing

Experiment 1: Simulated Annealing and varying period length

In Experiment 1, we were interested in the effects of varying the period length of a generator on the Simulated Annealing heuristic. As our source of randomness, we used a Mersenne Twister where we artificially reduced the period length to values ranging from 1003 to 512009.

The period lengths were chosen as prime numbers because we wanted to prevent moving in cycles as much as possible. Each run started at temperature 20. For each temperature, we executed 10000 iterations, then slightly decreased the actual temperature by multiplying it with the factor 0.97. The program ended after 100 different temperature values had been used. For each pseudorandom generator we used, the algorithm was run with 50 different seeds.

The pseudorandom numbers were used at two places: To compute a random neighbor permutation, we randomly swapped two elements of the current permutation, and to compute if a new permutation is accepted, we drew a

5.3 Experimental Setup and Results

	M. Twister 1	M. Twister 2	Quantum 1	Quantum 2	Diehard 1	Diehard 2	Trivium 1	Trivium 2
r-1009 vs. r-2003	×	×	×	×	×	×	×	×
r-2003 vs. r-4001	×	×	×	×	×	×	×	×
r-4001 vs. r-8009	×	×	×	×	×	×	×	×
r-8009 vs. r-16001	×	0.007	0.163	0.03	×	×	×	×
r-16001 vs. r-32003	0.107	0.025	0.5	0.002	0.212	0.288	×	0.031
r-32003 vs. r-64007	0.352	0.19	0.767	0.17	0.264	×	0.039	0.45
r-64007 vs. r-128021	0.203	0.233	0.061	0.543	0.333	0.977	0.53	0.632
r-128021 vs. r-256019	0.841	0.288	0.759	0.286	0.112	0.129	0.947	0.091
r-256019 vs. r-512009	0.274	0.378	0.603	0.31	0.737	0.28	0.39	0.32
r-512009 vs. MT	0.792	0.649	0.748	0.873	0.743	0.512	0.127	0.35
r-8009 vs. Q	×	×	0.354	×	×	×	×	×
r-16001 vs. Q	0.004	×	0.726	×	0.008	0.005	×	0.005
r-32003 vs. Q	0.095	0.113	0.724	0.432	0.058	0.019	0.291	0.324
r-64007 vs. Q	0.159	0.384	0.463	0.808	0.146	0.907	0.903	0.378
r-128021 vs. Q	0.415	0.681	0.916	0.773	0.271	0.244	0.896	0.238
r-256019 vs. Q	0.124	0.846	0.756	0.91	0.718	0.66	0.334	0.784
r-512009 vs. Q	0.225	0.908	0.668	0.963	0.496	0.831	0.442	0.908
MT vs. Q	0.083	0.86	0.413	0.766	0.269	0.827	0.847	0.969

Table 5.1: The p-values of the one-sided t test of Experiment 1. Values marked with × were smaller than 0.001. Column headers denote which input matrix was used. The alternative hypothesis for lines denoted with "A vs. B" was "Using generator A results in a higher average solution than using generator B".

5 Local and population based search heuristics

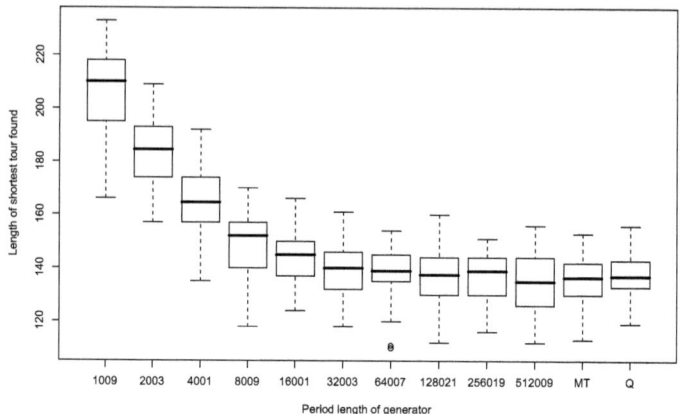

Figure 5.8: Simulated Annealing and the Traveling Salesman Problem (Experiment 1). Horizontal axis: Generator used. Vertical axis: Length of the shortest tour found with the help of that generator. For further parameters, see Table 5.2.

random number in the interval $[0, 1)$ and tested if that number was smaller than $e^{-\Delta f/T}$.

The optimal tour lengths we achieved for one of the inputs can be seen in Figure 5.8. Increasing the period length had a remarkable effect on the quality of our solutions. Note that the total number of random numbers that were used in each run lies between 3,000,000 and 3,100,000.

Looking at the p-values of Table 5.1 reveals that period lengths up to 16000 led to a significantly worse solution. This is not only shown by directly comparing the corresponding generator with the quantum generator, but also by comparing the generators with low period length with the generator with the next higher period length. In other words: Doubling the period length already had a visible effect.

5.3 Experimental Setup and Results

Parameter	Value
Heuristic	Simulated Annealing
Input	8 symmetric 50 × 50 distance matrices
Run time	100 temperature values, 10000 iterations per temperature
Generators	Mersenne Twister with reduced period length (denoted by r-x with x=period length)
Seeds per generator	50

Table 5.2: Parameters of Experiment 1.

Experiment 2: Simulated Annealing with a varying number of bits per number

In Experiment 2, we ran the Simulated Annealing heuristic with three different bit sources: The quantum generator, the Diehard sequence and the Trivium stream cipher. Our original goal was to investigate if any of these generators produces better resp. worse results than the others. Note that for the Diehard and Trivium sequence, even a better-than average result would imply some deficit in the sequence – they were both designed to "behave" like a random sequence, and causing a better result than a random sequence would make them distinguishable from a truly random source.

Parameter	Value
Heuristic	Simulated Annealing
Input	8 symmetric 50 × 50 distance matrices
Run time	100 temperature values, 10000 iterations per temperature
Generators	Numbers constructed from 8, 10, 12 or 16 bits of a random bit source. D-k denotes bits from the Diehard sequence, Q-K denotes bits from a quantum generator and T-k denotes bits from the Trivium stream cipher.
Seeds per generator	50

Table 5.3: Parameters of Experiment 2.

For each of the three bit sources, we created sequences of numbers in $[0,1)$ with four different block sizes: For $k \in \{8, 10, 12, 16\}$, we interpreted blocks of k bits as numbers in $\{0, 1, \ldots, 2^k - 1\}$, and divided these numbers by 2^k to map them to the interval $[0, 1)$.

99

5 Local and population based search heuristics

	M. Twister 1	M. Twister 2	Quantum 1	Quantum 2	Diehard 1	Diehard 2	Trivium 1	Trivium 2
Q-8 vs. Q	×	×	×	×	×	×	×	×
Q-10 vs. Q	×	×	×	×	×	×	×	×
Q-12 vs. Q	×	×	×	×	×	×	×	×
D-8 vs. Q	×	×	×	×	×	×	×	×
D-10 vs. Q	×	×	×	×	×	×	×	×
D-12 vs. Q	×	×	×	×	×	×	×	×
D-16 vs. Q	0.566	0.333	0.79	0.932	0.539	0.372	0.422	0.908
T-8 vs. Q	×	×	×	×	×	×	×	×
T-10 vs. Q	×	×	×	×	×	×	×	×
T-12 vs. Q	×	×	0.049	×	×	×	×	×
T-16 vs. Q	0.996	0.841	0.637	0.584	0.396	0.872	0.622	0.252
Q-8 vs. D-8	0.277	0.644	0.662	0.941	0.645	0.048	0.466	0.468
Q-8 vs. T-8	0.077	0.967	0.787	0.367	0.861	0.081	0.549	0.869
D-8 vs. T-8	0.711	0.661	0.883	0.481	0.519	0.82	0.916	0.338
Q-10 vs. D-10	0.617	0.45	0.469	0.103	0.739	0.624	0.35	0.567
Q-10 vs. T-10	0.066	0.434	0.379	0.725	0.694	0.271	0.036	0.393
D-10 vs. T-10	0.016	0.164	0.898	0.071	0.96	0.547	0.25	0.142
Q-12 vs. D-12	0.832	0.674	0.635	0.429	0.471	0.822	0.375	0.035
Q-12 vs. T-12	0.798	0.109	0.017	0.72	0.728	0.301	0.431	0.087
D-12 vs. T-12	0.601	0.231	0.015	0.638	0.634	0.101	0.899	0.624
Q-16 vs. D-16	0.859	0.447	0.517	0.884	0.461	0.876	0.129	0.033
Q-16 vs. T-16	0.012	0.562	0.307	0.288	0.267	0.139	0.234	0.741
D-16 vs. T-16	0.046	0.211	0.671	0.311	0.758	0.25	0.66	0.08

Table 5.4: The p-values of Experiment 2. Values marked with × were smaller than 0.001. A row designated with "G-k vs. Q" contains the p-values of a one-sided t test with the alternative hypothesis "Source G with blocks of k bits leads to a larger average result than the quantum generator with blocks of 16 bits". Analogously, lines denoted "G_1-k vs. G_2-k" corresponds to a one-sided t test with alternative hypothesis "Source G_1 with blocks of k bits leads to a larger average result than source G_2 with blocks of k bits".

5.3 Experimental Setup and Results

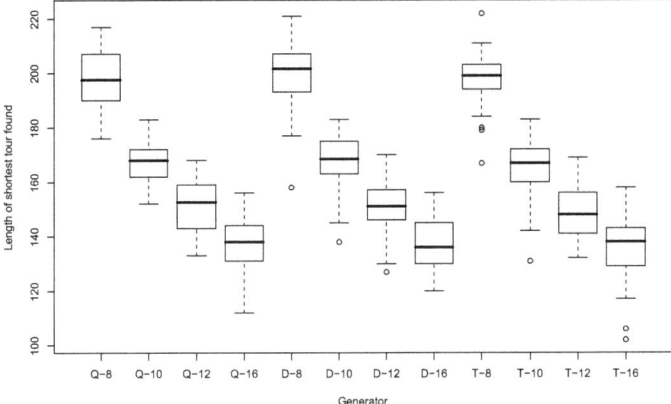

Figure 5.9: Simulated Annealing and the Traveling Salesman Problem with three different bit sources, limited to different numbers of bits per random number (Experiment 2). Horizontal axis: Generator used. Vertical axis: Length of the shortest tour found with the help of that generator. For further parameters, see Table 5.3.

A difference between the three sources could not be observed. However, another connection was discovered: The number of bits that were used to create a random number significantly determined the quality of the solution. A representative plot for one of the input matrices can be seen in Figure 5.9. With equal block sizes, the actual bit source did not matter, and all three sources led to very similar results. However, a lower number of bits caused Simulated Annealing to produce worse results, independently from the bit source.

Experiment 3: Simulated Annealing and a biased random bit source

In Experiment 3, we wanted to find out if a biased source of random bits could influence the output of Simulated Annealing. We again used the heuristic to solve the Traveling Salesman Problem instances described above (see Experiment 1). As our source of randomness, we used the Mersenne Twister and produced biased numbers in the following way: During each run, we specified

5 Local and population based search heuristics

the probability p to obtain a 0 bit. We then drew 12 random numbers in the interval $[0,1)$. Each number smaller than p resulted in a 0, each number greater than or equal to p resulted in a 1. Those 12 bits were then interpreted as a binary number in $[0,1)$ and passed to the algorithm.

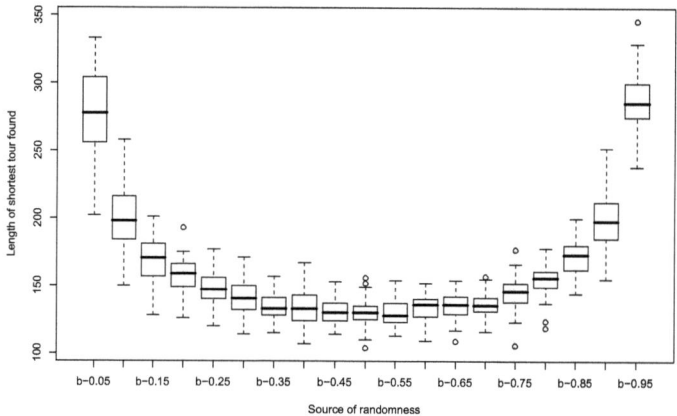

Figure 5.10: Simulated Annealing and the Traveling Salesman Problem with a biased bit source (Experiment 3). Horizontal axis: Generator used. Vertical axis: Length of the shortest tour found with the help of that generator. For further parameters, see Table 5.6.

The parameters for this experiment can be found in Table 5.6.

The optimal tour lengths we achieved can be seen in Figure 5.10. Table 5.5 shows the p-values obtained with the one-sided t-test and the alternative hypothesis "The biased source leads to a higher average result than the non-biased source". When the probability for a 0 was increased or decreased by 0.1, a total of 4 out of 16 p-values were smaller than 0.05, a sign that a bias of 0.1 already leads to a slight deterioration of the result. A stronger bias showed a definite increase in the average solution – When increasing or decreasing the probability of a 0 by 0.15 or more, the p-values remained almost consistently below 0.05.

	M. Twister 1	M. Twister 2	Quantum 1	Quantum 2	Diehard 1	Diehard 2	Trivium 1	Trivium 2
b-0.05	×	×	×	×	×	×	×	×
b-0.1	×	×	×	×	×	×	×	×
b-0.15	×	×	×	×	×	×	×	×
b-0.2	×	×	×	×	×	×	×	×
b-0.25	×	×	×	×	×	×	×	×
b-0.3	×	×	0.001	×	×	×	×	×
b-0.35	0.01	0.02	0.042	×	0.003	×	0.046	0.014
b-0.4	0.228	0.081	0.461	0.038	0.418	0.128	0.975	0.713
b-0.45	0.538	0.255	0.986	0.118	0.575	0.368	0.6	0.235
b-0.5	0.5	0.5	0.5	0.5	0.5	0.5	0.5	0.5
b-0.55	0.718	0.437	0.28	0.374	0.306	0.053	0.534	0.587
b-0.6	0.184	0.014	0.105	0.033	0.114	0.01	0.402	0.408
b-0.65	0.008	0.004	0.506	×	0.017	0.001	0.066	0.059
b-0.7	0.001	×	×	0.003	×	×	0.012	×
b-0.75	×	×	×	×	×	×	×	×
b-0.8	×	×	×	×	×	×	×	×
b-0.85	×	×	×	×	×	×	×	×
b-0.9	×	×	×	×	×	×	×	×
b-0.95	×	×	×	×	×	×	×	×

Table 5.5: The p-values of Experiment 3. Values marked with × were smaller than 0.001. *b-x* denotes a generator with a probability of *x* to output a 0 bit. For each random number, 12 of these bits were combined.

5 Local and population based search heuristics

Parameter	Value
Heuristic	Simulated Annealing
Input	8 symmetric 50 × 50 distance matrices
Run time	100 temperature values, 10000 iterations per temperature
Generators	Biased numbers constructed from 12 biased bits (b-p denotes that each bit was equal to 0 with probability p)
Seeds per generator	50

Table 5.6: Parameters of Experiment 3.

Experiment 4: Simulated Annealing and quasi-random sequences

In Experiment 4, the Simulated Annealing heuristic was again used to solve an instance of the Traveling Salesman Problem. Initial temperature and cooling schedule were the same as in Experiment 1.

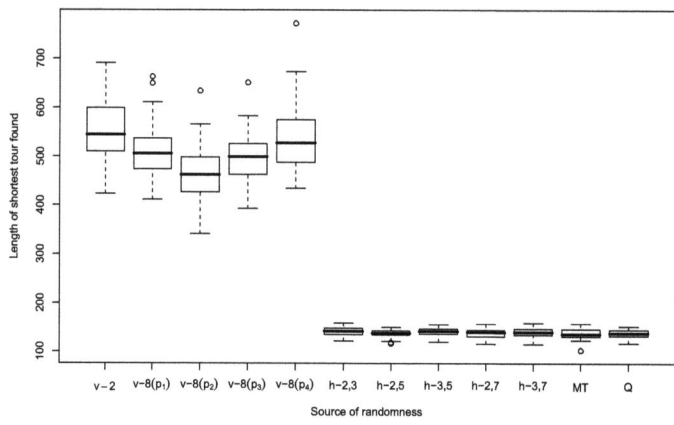

Figure 5.11: Traveling Salesman Problem with Simulated Annealing and quasirandom sequences (Experiment 4). Horizontal axis: Pseudorandom number generator we used. Vertical axis: Length of the shortest tour found with the help of that generator. For further parameters, see Table 5.8.

	M. Twister 1	M. Twister 2	Quantum 1	Quantum 2	Diehard 1	Diehard 2	Trivium 1	Trivium 2
vdc2	×	×	×	×	×	×	×	×
vdc8p1	×	×	×	×	×	×	×	×
vdc8p2	×	×	×	×	×	×	×	×
vdc8p3	×	×	×	×	×	×	×	×
vdc8p4	×	×	×	×	×	×	×	×
hal2-23	×	0.076	0.034	0.029	0.005	×	0.01	0.005
hal2-25	0.003	0.675	0.072	0.02	×	×	0.054	0.011
hal2-35	0.003	0.019	0.006	0.002	×	0.001	0.01	×
hal2-27	0.003	0.413	0.059	0.004	0.004	0.128	×	×
hal2-37	0.018	0.16	×	0.01	0.002	×	0.008	0.016
MT	0.012	0.713	0.07	0.363	0.613	0.424	0.909	0.653

Table 5.7: The p-values of the one-sided t tests of Experiment 4. Values marked with × were smaller than 0.001

This time we used van der Corput sequences and Halton sequences of dimension 2 as sources of randomness. Each of the van der Corput and Halton sequences was started at 50 different points, the Mersenne Twister was used with 50 different seeds. Since the roulette wheel algorithm does not need tuples from the random source, we used the Halton sequences in a simplified way and flattened them: Let $((x_{11}, x_{12}), (x_{21}, x_{22}), (x_{31}, x_{32}), \ldots)$ be a Halton sequence of dimension 2. Then we used the 1-dimensional sequence $(x_{11}, x_{12}, x_{21}, x_{22}, x_{31}, \ldots)$ instead. For the van der Corput sequences in base 8, we additionally permuted the digits of n, i.e. instead of ϕ_b in Definition 17, we used

$$\tilde{\phi}_b(n) = \sum_{j=0}^{\infty} p(n_i) b^{-i-1} ,$$

where p was a permutation of $\{0, \ldots, 7\}$. We used the permutations
$p_1 = (2\ 4\ 6\ 0\ 1\ 3\ 5\ 7)$,
$p_2 = (0\ 3\ 6\ 1\ 4\ 7\ 2\ 5)$,
$p_3 = (2\ 5\ 6\ 4\ 1\ 0\ 3\ 7)$ and
$p_4 = (3\ 6\ 4\ 5\ 1\ 7\ 2\ 0)$
(meaning that p_1 maps 0 to 2, 1 to 4, 2 to 6, ...), as described in [25].

5 Local and population based search heuristics

Parameter	Value
Heuristic	Simulated Annealing
Input	symmetric 50 × 50 distance matrix
Run time	100 temperature values, 10000 iterations per temperature
Generators	van der Corput sequences of base 2 (vdc2) van der Corput sequences of base 8 (vdc8-px) 2-dimensional Halton sequences (Hal-xy) Mersenne Twister (MT)
Seeds per generator	50

Table 5.8: Parameters of Experiment 4.

The results of Experiment 4 can be seen in Figure 5.11. Here, "v-2" denotes the van der Corput sequence in base 2, "v-8(p_1)" to "v-8(p_4)" denote van der Corput sequences in base 8, with permutations 1 to 4, and sources beginning with "h-" denote different Halton sequences.

With the use of van der Corput sequences, the algorithm consistently found worse solutions than with the Mersenne Twister, whereas the use of Mersenne Twister and Halton sequences both led to good solutions. When we compare the means with the help of a t test and take a closer look at the p-values (see Table 5.7), only the Mersenne Twister shows non-suspicious p-values, while the Halton sequences lead to many p-values around 0.01, a sign that they probably lead to worse solutions.

Experiment 5: Simulated Annealing and k-wise independence

In Experiment 5, we tried to measure the influence of k-wise independence on the quality of the Simulated Annealing heuristic. We fixed the range m of an explicit polynomial generator at $m = 1000$ and varied its degree from $k = 2$ up to $k = 8$.

To find good coefficient sets for that generator, we used the following approach: For each degree k, we created 200 coefficient sets at random, i.e. we chose the coefficients $a_0, \ldots, a_k$. For each of these coefficient sets, we then output 100000 numbers with a polynomial generator that used these coefficients. Each of these output sequences was then compressed individually with the bzip2 algorithm.

5.3 Experimental Setup and Results

Parameter	Value
Heuristic	Simulated Annealing
Input	symmetric 50×50 distance matrix
Run time	100 temperature values, 10000 iterations per temperature
Generators	Polynomial generators with period length 10000 and degree $k \in \{2, \ldots, 10\}$ (denoted by p-k) Mersenne Twister
Seeds per generator	60 (20 for each parameter set)

Table 5.9: Parameters of Experiment 5.

	M. Twister 1	M. Twister 2	Quantum 1	Quantum 2	Diehard 1	Diehard 2	Trivium 1	Trivium 2
poly-2 vs. Q	×	×	×	×	×	×	×	×
poly-4 vs. Q	×	×	×	×	×	×	×	×
poly-6 vs. Q	×	×	×	×	×	×	×	×
poly-8 vs. Q	×	×	×	×	×	×	×	×
poly-2b vs. Q	×	×	0.002	×	×	×	×	×
poly-4b vs. Q	0.59	0.245	0.393	0.225	0.096	0.084	0.678	0.232
poly-6b vs. Q	0.205	0.252	0.391	0.48	0.03	0.099	0.953	0.682
poly-8b vs. Q	0.667	0.598	0.391	0.07	0.003	0.275	0.638	0.491

Table 5.10: The p-values of the one-sided t tests of Experiment 5. Values marked with × were smaller than 0.001.

For our experiment, we only chose the three coefficient sets that led to the three longest files after compression. That way, we tried to avoid sequences with obvious regularities.

Most other parameters were chosen as for Experiment 1. For an overview of the parameters, see Table 5.9.

The results of the experiment are detailed in Table 5.10, a representative plot is shown in Figure 5.12. Increasing the degree of the polynomial generator did not significantly increase the quality of the solution. Comparing with the results of Experiment 1, the solutions achieved with the polynomial generators are comparable to those achived when using a pseudorandom generator with

5 Local and population based search heuristics

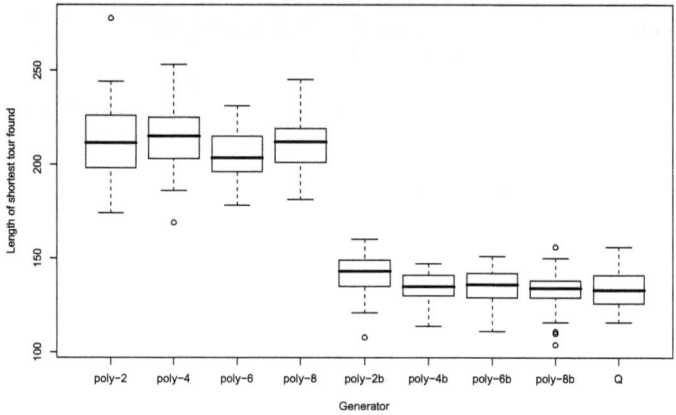

Figure 5.12: Traveling Salesman Problem with Simulated Annealing and polynomial generators (Experiment 5). Horizontal axis: Pseudorandom number generator we used. Vertical axis: Length of the shortest tour found with the help of that generator. For further parameters, see Table 5.9.

period length of 1000 – a two-sided t test that compared the results for the polynomial generators with the results for the Mersenne Twister with reduced period length of 1009 didn't result in a suspicious p-value. Since our polynomial generators had a modulus $m = 1000$, and thus a period length of 1000, period length seems to have more influence on the result than k-wise independence of the pseudorandom numbers.

Experiment 6: Simulated Annealing and DeJong's test functions

In Experiment 6, we tested the performance of Simulated Annealing on DeJong's suite of test functions. In order to get more distinctive results, we used versions of these functions with relatively high dimensions: For functions f_1, f_3, f_4 and f_5, we used dimension 20. For f_2, dimension 2 was sufficient.

The Simulated Annealing heuristic started at temperature 20. For some common

5.3 Experimental Setup and Results

Parameter	Value
Heuristic	Simulated Annealing
Run time	100 temperature values, 500 iterations per temperature
Generators	Mersenne Twister with reduced period length (denoted by r-x), van der Corput sequences (denoted by vdc...) Halton sequences of dimensions 2 (denoted by hal2-x) and 20 (denoted by hal20)
Seeds per generator	50

Table 5.11: Parameters of Experiment 6.

	f_1	f_2	f_3	f_4	f_5
vdc2 vs. r-512009	×	×	×	0.454	0.58
vdc8p1 vs. r-512009	×	×	×	0.937	×
vdc8p2 vs. r-512009	0.003	×	×	×	×
vdc8p3 vs. r-512009	0.042	×	×	0.989	×
vdc8p4 vs. r-512009	1	0.955	×	0.984	×
hal2-23 vs. r-512009	×	×	×	0.176	×
hal2-25 vs. r-512009	1	0.832	×	0.859	×
hal2-35 vs. r-512009	×	×	×	0.747	×
hal20 vs. r-512009	0.215	0.117	0.003	×	0.335
r-1009 vs. r-512009	0.052	0.115	×	×	0.16
r-2003 vs. r-512009	0.112	0.025	×	×	0.734
r-4001 vs. r-512009	0.17	0.039	×	×	0.645
r-8009 vs. r-512009	0.19	0.13	×	×	0.933
r-16001 vs. r-512009	0.182	0.27	×	×	0.578
r-32003 vs. r-512009	0.433	0.25	0.003	×	0.501
r-64007 vs. r-512009	0.095	0.133	×	×	0.606
r-128021 vs. r-512009	0.177	0.582	0.028	×	0.177
r-256019 vs. r-512009	0.02	0.799	0.108	0.001	0.263

Table 5.12: The p-values of the one-sided t test of Experiment 6. Values marked with × were smaller than 0.001.

parameters of this experiment, see Table 5.11. To obtain a neighbor of the actual state, we changed every component of the current vector by a pseudorandom number that was Gaussian distributed with mean 0 and standard deviation 0.02 times the range of the function's domain. Such a number was created by drawing a uniformly distributed number in the interval $[0,1)$ and applying the inverse probability function of the normal distribution on that number. As

5 Local and population based search heuristics

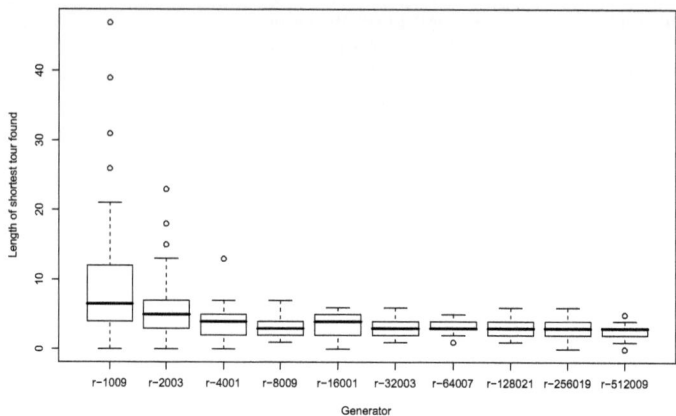

Figure 5.13: Solving DeJong's test function f_3 with Simulated Annealing (Experiment 6). Horizontal axis: Generator used. Vertical axis: Minimum value of f_3 found with the help of that generator. For further parameters, see Table 5.11.

the source of randomness we used the modified Mersenne Twister, where the period length was artificially reduced to values ranging from 1003 to 512009, as well as van der Corput and Halton sequences with several different bases. Three of the Halton sequences had dimension 2, whereas one had dimension 20, using the first 20 primes as bases. As in Experiment 1, we used primes as period lengths for the reduced Mersenne Twister to avoid moving in cycles. For each run we measured the minimum function value the Simulated Annealing heuristic found in the specified domain.

A representative plot of this experiment can be seen in Figure 5.13, where f_3 is solved with the help of a Mersenne Twister with artificially reduced period length. The p-values of this experiment can be seen in Table 5.12. Most of the quasi-random sequences are not suited for this kind of problem, and the generators with reduced period length caused difficulties to solve functions f_3 and f_4 and, to some extent, f_2. Even the Halton sequence of dimension 20 had problems with functions f_3 and f_4.

5.3 Experimental Setup and Results

These results indicate that the results of our previous experiments are not limited to the Traveling Salesman Problem, or the class of discrete optimization problems, but also applicable to the optimization of some continuous functions.

5.3.2 Population based heuristics

Experiment 7: A genetic algorithm with linear congruential generators

In Experiment 7 we ran a simple evolutionary algorithm on the same instance of the TSP problem as in Experiment 1. In each step, the fitness values of the population were calculated and the next population then chosen by a roulette wheel algorithm (see Listing 5.1 in Section 5.2). Then 50% of the population was mutated, switching two permutation elements. From this new population, we then created 10 new elements by combining two random elements with the edge-3 crossover operator [62]. These new elements replaced one of their parents each. The algorithm was run for 10000 generations. For each new generation, we made sure that the best element from the previous generation survived the selection procedure.

Parameter	Value
Heuristic	Evolutionary Algorithm
Input	8 symmetric 50×50 distance matrices
Population size	100
Run time	10000 iterations
Generators	linear congruential generators
	Mersenne Twister (MT)
	Quantum generator (Q)
Seeds per generator	60 (20 for each of three parameter sets for lcg)

Table 5.13: Parameters of Experiment 7.

As source of randomness, we used linear congruential generators that had maximum period lengths from 1000 up to 512000. Their parameters were chosen such that their output could not be well compressed by the bzip2 program. To this end, we randomly chose parameters that could guarantee maximum

5 Local and population based search heuristics

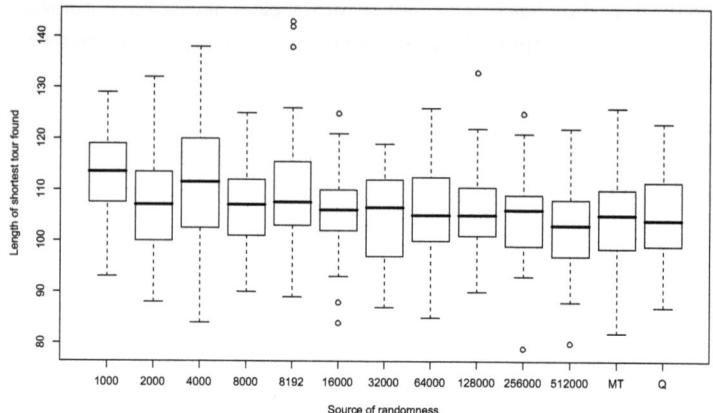

Figure 5.14: Solving the Traveling Salesman Problem with a population based approach (Experiment 7). Horizontal axis: Pseudorandom number generator we used (numbers denote the length of the linear congruential generator). Vertical axis: Length of the shortest tour found with the help of that generator. For further parameters, see Table 5.13.

period lengths, then saved sequences obtained from a linear congruential generator with these parameters and compressed the resulting file. For each period length, we used the three parameter sets that resulted in the 3 biggest files after compression. For each of these parameter sets, we used 20 different seeds. For comparison, we also used the Mersenne Twister and the quantum generator.

Figure 5.14 shows the results of this experiment, p-values obtained from a one-sided t test can be found in Table 5.14. Only generators with very short period lengths led to visibly worse results than the quantum generator. Note that the generator with period length 8192 was proposed by Kruskal in [65]. While it can be computed very fast on a 16 bit architecture, it doesn't seem to be well suited for a genetic algorithm, with p-values less than 0.05 for 5 of our 8 input matrices.

5.3 Experimental Setup and Results

	M. Twister 1	M. Twister 2	Quantum 1	Quantum 2	Diehard 1	Diehard 2	Trivium 1	Trivium 2
1-1000	×	×	×	0.012	×	×	×	0.073
1-2000	0.065	0.025	0.002	0.176	0.005	×	0.002	0.163
1-4000	×	×	0.001	0.005	×	×	×	0.004
1-8000	0.284	0.084	0.111	0.341	0.11	0.119	0.094	0.769
1-8192	0.194	0.002	0.147	0.375	0.033	×	0.008	0.045
1-16000	0.354	0.21	0.573	0.871	0.447	0.082	0.029	0.267
1-32000	0.614	0.392	0.071	0.737	0.56	0.049	0.221	0.828
1-64000	0.17	0.207	0.439	0.322	0.613	0.018	0.108	0.556
1-128000	0.21	0.12	0.953	0.459	0.295	0.291	0.076	0.792
1-256000	0.217	0.357	0.64	0.685	0.893	0.047	0.079	0.462
1-512000	0.071	0.887	0.527	0.673	0.335	0.361	0.284	0.425
MT	0.709	0.428	0.29	0.598	0.264	0.398	0.129	0.442

Table 5.14: p-values of Experiment 7. Values marked with × were smaller than 0.001. Alternative hypothesis: "Using this generator leads to a higher average solution than using the quantum generator."

Experiment 8: A genetic algorithm with a varying number of bits per random number

In Experiment 8 we used different numbers of bits to create our random numbers, analogously to Experiment 2. Remember that the number of bits used to compose the random numbers had a very large effect on the Simulated Annealing heuristic.

In contrast, the number of bits we used did not have a visible effect on the length of the best tour the Genetic Algorithm found. Figure 5.15 shows a representative plot, with the second input matrix we created with the Mersenne Twister, the same input matrix that is shown for the other experiments. See also the table of p-values (Table 5.16) for that experiment – for the other input matrices, comparing two sequences generated from the same number of bits never led to a p-value below 0.03. So the results for the quantum generator combining 16 bits should probably be considered an outlier.

	M. Twister 1	M. Twister 2	Quantum 1	Quantum 2	Diehard 1	Diehard 2	Trivium 1	Trivium 2
Q-8 vs. Q	0.047	0.338	0.244	0.854	0.831	0.172	0.914	0.794
Q-10 vs. Q	0.742	0.015	0.578	0.847	0.463	0.379	0.955	0.739
Q-12 vs. Q	0.186	0.824	0.245	0.644	0.361	0.065	0.261	0.989
Q-16 vs. Q	0.037	0.003	0.518	0.171	0.944	0.088	0.691	0.448
D-8 vs. Q	0.214	0.6	0.22	0.933	0.922	0.153	0.39	0.668
D-10 vs. Q	0.599	0.069	0.358	0.866	0.915	0.62	0.427	0.901
D-12 vs. Q	0.464	0.518	0.797	0.837	0.438	0.141	0.6	0.544
D-16 vs. Q	0.488	0.548	0.364	0.731	0.039	0.174	0.491	0.976
T-8 vs. Q	0.341	0.098	0.634	0.636	0.36	0.297	0.849	0.543
T-10 vs. Q	0.358	0.221	0.344	0.168	0.177	0.095	0.494	0.683
T-12 vs. Q	0.582	0.693	0.067	0.295	0.538	0.168	0.211	0.459
T-16 vs. Q	0.352	0.872	0.392	0.859	0.803	0.253	0.714	0.325
Q-8 vs. D-8	0.41	0.57	0.889	0.659	0.771	0.992	0.158	0.76
Q-8 vs. T-8	0.251	0.498	0.367	0.629	0.28	0.676	0.693	0.537
D-8 vs. T-8	0.734	0.188	0.337	0.396	0.154	0.663	0.265	0.772
Q-10 vs. D-10	0.72	0.559	0.634	0.913	0.224	0.602	0.106	0.494
Q-10 vs. T-10	0.384	0.221	0.611	0.076	0.483	0.359	0.119	0.877
D-10 vs. T-10	0.593	0.529	0.966	0.069	0.051	0.172	0.875	0.411
Q-12 vs. D-12	0.437	0.458	0.194	0.611	0.864	0.721	0.414	0.056
Q-12 vs. T-12	0.326	0.756	0.429	0.443	0.704	0.624	0.824	0.03
D-12 vs. T-12	0.784	0.692	0.05	0.193	0.829	0.901	0.339	0.852
Q-16 vs. D-16	0.095	0.016	0.744	0.194	0.005	0.621	0.668	0.058
Q-16 vs. T-16	0.189	×	0.792	0.087	0.58	0.535	0.983	0.762
D-16 vs. T-16	0.74	0.395	0.939	0.753	0.026	0.863	0.638	0.038

Table 5.15: p-values of Experiment 8. Values marked with × were smaller than 0.001. Alternative hypothesis: "Using this generator leads to a higher average solution than when using the quantum generator."

5.3 Experimental Setup and Results

Parameter	Value
Heuristic	Evolutionary Algorithm
Input	8 symmetric 50×50 distance matrices
Population size	100
Run time	10000 iterations
Generators	Random bit sources Trivium, Diehard and the quantum generator, with 8,10,12 and 16 bits combined to create random numbers.
Seeds per generator	50

Table 5.16: Parameters of Experiment 8.

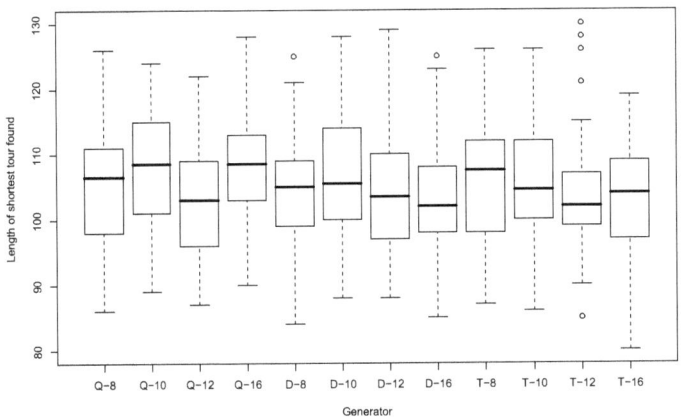

Figure 5.15: Solving the Traveling Salesman Problem with a population based approach (Experiment 8). Horizontal axis: Pseudorandom number generator we used. Vertical axis: Length of the shortest tour found with the help of that generator. For further parameters, see Table 5.16.

Experiment 9: A genetic algorithm and a biased source of random bits

Compared to Simulated Annealing, the genetic algorithm found quite good solutions when using generators with short period length. So one might also expect some kind of robustness when using a biased source of random bits. So we ran the genetic algorithm on our 8 distance matrices of the Traveling

5 Local and population based search heuristics

Salesman Problem.

Parameter	Value
Heuristic	Evolutionary Algorithm
Input	8 symmetric 50 × 50 distance matrices
Population size	100
Run time	10000 iterations
Generators	Biased numbers constructed from 12 biased bits (b-p denotes that each bit was equal to 0 with probability p)
Seeds per generator	50

Table 5.17: Parameters of Experiment 9.

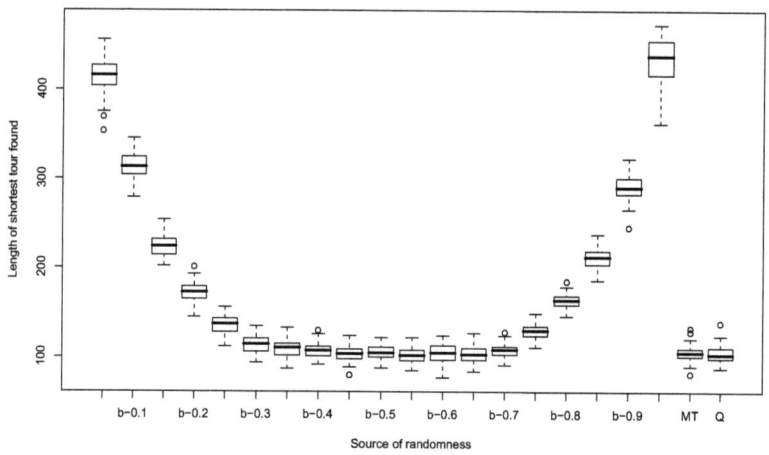

Figure 5.16: Solving the Traveling Salesman Problem with a population based approach (Experiment 9). Horizontal axis: Pseudorandom number generator we used. Vertical axis: Length of the shortest tour found with the help of that generator. For further parameters, see Table 5.17.

For parameters, see Table 5.17. A plot for one of the matrices is shown as Figure 5.16. A slight bias of only 0.05 increased the output noticeably only for 3 out of 16 cases, indicated by a p-value less than 0.05 when comparing the result with the quantum generator via a one-sided t test. Increasing the bias beyond 0.05

	M. Twister 1	M. Twister 2	Quantum 1	Quantum 2	Diehard 1	Diehard 2	Trivium 1	Trivium 2
b-0.05	×	×	×	×	×	×	×	×
b-0.1	×	×	×	×	×	×	×	×
b-0.15	×	×	×	×	×	×	×	×
b-0.2	×	×	×	×	×	×	×	×
b-0.25	×	×	×	×	×	×	×	×
b-0.3	×	×	×	×	×	×	×	×
b-0.35	×	0.018	0.047	×	0.262	0.001	0.013	×
b-0.4	0.023	0.072	0.37	0.343	0.634	0.116	0.085	0.003
b-0.45	0.039	0.735	0.587	0.512	0.954	0.016	0.34	0.301
b-0.5	0.113	0.482	0.824	0.314	0.976	0.073	0.468	0.776
b-0.55	0.027	0.869	0.996	0.759	0.828	0.211	0.954	0.492
b-0.6	0.903	0.532	0.979	0.933	0.895	0.431	0.841	0.602
b-0.65	0.609	0.565	0.946	0.986	0.911	0.512	0.961	0.885
b-0.7	0.008	0.043	0.058	0.104	0.4	0.009	0.028	0.002
b-0.75	×	×	×	×	×	×	×	×
b-0.8	×	×	×	×	×	×	×	×
b-0.85	×	×	×	×	×	×	×	×
b-0.9	×	×	×	×	×	×	×	×
b-0.95	×	×	×	×	×	×	×	×

Table 5.18: The p-values of the one-sided t test of Experiment 9. Values marked with × were smaller than 0.001.

5 Local and population based search heuristics

showed an effect similar to Experiment 3, where Simulated Annealing was used with a biased bit source.

Note that both Experiments 3 and 9 actually show a positive result: A bias of 0.05 is already quite high and combining 12 of these biased bits results in a distribution far from a uniform distribution. In practice, any good pseudorandom generator should show a distribution much closer to the uniform distribution. The bias of a lagged fibonacci generator shown in [27], for example, is much smaller. On the other hand, the bias of a simple pseudorandom generator, like the linear congruential generator, can easily surpass 0.05 when considering the *conditional* probability to obtain a given number: In [50], a worst case for the QuickSort algorithm was constructed where 25% of all seeds led to almost the same situation, with the same current state of the random generator. It might also be possible to create such a worst case scenario for a search heuristic like a Genetic Algorithm, or Simulated Annealing.

Experiment 10: A genetic algorithm and quasi-random sequences

In Experiment 10, we tried to solve the Traveling Salesman problem with the help of van der Corput sequences and Halton sequences of dimension 2 as sources of randomness. Since the mutation step needs two random numbers, quasi-random sequences of dimension 2 might look like an interesting tool, while we expected sequences of dimension 1 (in our case van der Corput sequences) to rather pose a problem to the genetic algorithm.

Parameter	Value
Heuristic	Evolutionary Algorithm
Input	symmetric 50 × 50 distance matrix
Population size	100
Run time	10,000 iterations
Generators	van der Corput sequences of base 2 (vdc2)
	van der Corput sequences of base 8 (vdc8-px)
	2-dimensional Halton sequences (hal-xy)
	Mersenne Twister (MT)
	Quantum generator
Seeds per generator	50

Table 5.19: Parameters of Experiment 10.

5.3 Experimental Setup and Results

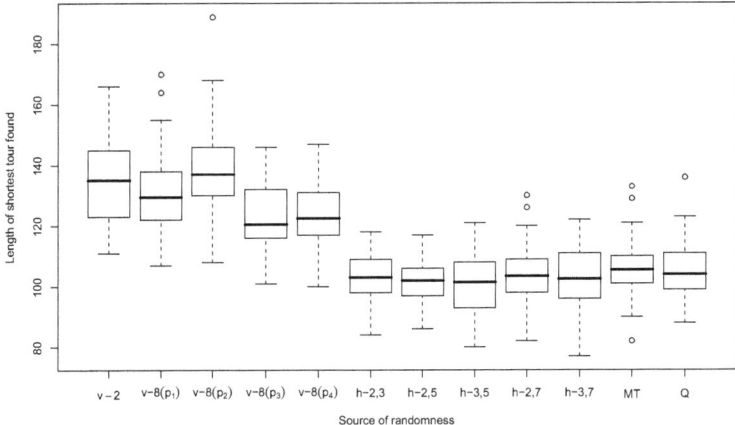

Figure 5.17: Solving the TSP with a population based approach, using quasi-random sequences (Experiment 10). Horizontal axis: Pseudorandom number generator we used. Vertical axis: Length of the shortest tour found with the help of that generator. For further parameters, see Table 5.19.

Since the roulette wheel algorithm needs single numbers instead of tuples from the random source, we flattened the Halton sequences as described in Experiment 4. The van der Corput sequences in base 8 used permutations, see Experiment 4 for further details.

The results of Experiment 10 for one of the inputs can be seen in Figure 5.17, the p-values obtained with the one-sided t test, comparing each generator with the quantum generator, can be seen in Table 5.20. Additionally, we also tested if the Halton sequences led to a *better* result than the quantum generator. First of all: The genetic algorithm seems to be much less effected by the usage of van der Corput sequences. For comparison, see Figure 5.11 and Table 5.7, which show a Simulated Annealing heuristic with the same task of solving the TSP with quasi-random sequences. Simulated Annealing had much larger problems with pseudorandom numbers that do not spread well in 2 dimensions. In addition, note that running the genetic algorithm with 2-dimensional Halton

119

5 Local and population based search heuristics

	M. Twister 1	M. Twister 2	Quantum 1	Quantum 2	Diehard 1	Diehard 2	Trivium 1	Trivium 2
vdc2 vs. Q	×	×	×	×	×	×	×	×
vdc8p1 vs. Q	×	×	×	×	×	×	×	×
vdc8p2 vs. Q	×	×	×	×	×	×	×	×
vdc8p3 vs. Q	×	×	×	×	×	×	×	×
vdc8p4 vs. Q	×	×	×	×	×	×	×	×
hal2-23 vs. Q	0.883	0.957	0.938	0.907	0.984	0.99	0.998	0.972
hal2-25 vs. Q	0.781	0.975	0.981	0.991	0.947	0.987	0.998	0.954
hal2-35 vs. Q	0.613	0.989	0.994	0.84	0.881	0.89	0.96	0.995
hal2-27 vs. Q	0.839	0.772	0.94	0.988	0.996	0.991	0.999	0.974
hal2-37 vs. Q	0.855	0.797	0.985	0.916	0.94	0.998	0.996	0.989
MT vs. Q	0.51	0.47	0.834	0.658	0.128	0.745	0.656	0.739
Q vs. hal2-23	0.117	0.043	0.062	0.093	0.016	0.01	0.002	0.028
Q vs. hal2-25	0.219	0.025	0.019	0.009	0.053	0.013	0.002	0.046
Q vs. hal2-35	0.387	0.011	0.006	0.16	0.119	0.11	0.04	0.005
Q vs. hal2-27	0.161	0.228	0.06	0.012	0.004	0.009	0.001	0.026
Q vs. hal2-37	0.145	0.203	0.015	0.084	0.06	0.002	0.004	0.011

Table 5.20: The p-values of Experiment 10. Values marked with × were smaller than 0.001. "vdc" denotes a van der Corput sequence, "hal" a Halton sequence, "MT" the Mersenne Twister and "Q" the quantum generator.

sequences led to results that were even slightly better than those obtained with the quantum generator, leading to many p-values at or below 0.01.

Experiment 11: Using quasi-random sequences for different steps

In Experiment 11, we wanted to find an explanation why the use of van der Corput sequences in Experiment 10 led to worse solutions. Particularly, we wanted to know which of the steps in the Genetic Algorithm suffered from using quasirandom sequences – crossover, mutation or selection via the roulette wheel. To this end, we separately provided the roulette wheel algorithm and the mutation resp. crossover steps with van der Corput sequences while providing the other parts with numbers from the Mersenne Twister.

5.3 Experimental Setup and Results

	M. Twister 1	M. Twister 2	Quantum 1	Quantum 2	Diehard 1	Diehard 2	Trivium 1	Trivium 2
M-vdc2	×	×	×	×	×	×	×	×
M-vdc8p1	×	×	×	×	×	×	×	×
M-vdc8p2	×	×	×	×	×	×	×	×
M-vdc8p3	×	×	×	×	×	×	×	×
M-vdc8p4	×	×	×	×	×	×	×	×
C-vdc2	0.539	0.305	0.868	0.289	0.033	0.492	0.514	0.304
C-vdc8p1	0.474	0.548	0.655	0.224	0.019	0.676	0.22	0.727
C-vdc8p2	0.957	0.787	0.809	0.326	0.182	0.657	0.458	0.667
C-vdc8p3	0.689	0.715	0.433	0.088	0.206	0.854	0.423	0.8
C-vdc8p4	0.828	0.691	0.487	0.682	0.372	0.789	0.221	0.152
R-vdc2	0.91	0.906	0.923	0.869	0.78	0.433	0.718	0.681
R-vdc8p1	0.9	0.992	0.872	0.491	0.961	0.542	0.798	0.423
R-vdc8p2	0.93	0.93	0.995	0.967	0.885	0.918	0.969	0.874
R-vdc8p3	0.982	0.999	0.859	0.981	0.98	0.482	0.76	0.809
R-vdc8p4	0.939	0.992	0.917	0.606	0.926	0.971	0.746	0.491

Table 5.21: p-values of Experiment 11. Values marked with × were smaller than 0.001. M-X denotes cases where the mutation step was provided with sequence X. Analogously, C-X denotes cases where the crossover step used sequence X and R-X denotes cases where the roulette wheel algorithm used sequence X. The other parts used the Mersenne Twister.

5 Local and population based search heuristics

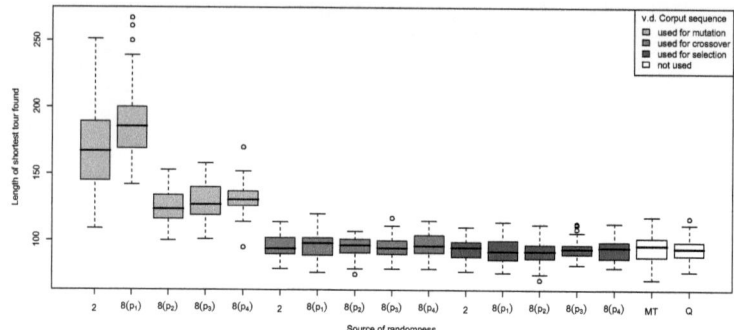

Figure 5.18: A population based approach, using different pseudorandom generators (quasirandom sequences and a Mersenne Twister) for mutation, crossover and selection (Experiment 11). Horizontal axis: Pseudorandom number generator we used – 2 and 8 denote van der Corput sequences of bases 2 and 8 (with permutations p_1 to p_4), MT and Q denote Mersenne Twister and the Quantum Generator. Vertical axis: Length of the shortest tour found with the help of that combination of generators. For further parameters, see Table 5.22.

Note that in the Schema Theorem, only the selection procedure actively contributes to a constant shift towards a population with higher average fitness. Both crossover and mutation worsen the bound given in that theorem. However, they are necessary components that help move away from local optima. Additionally, the fact that these two components worsen the lower bound doesn't necessarily imply that they actually worsen the population's fitness.

A plot of the results of this experiment for one of the inputs can be seen in Figure 5.18, the p-values from the comparison with the quantum generator can be seen in Table 5.21. Only using van der Corput sequences in the mutation step led to worse results. Using them for the crossover or selection step did not result in any significant increase in the length of the shortest tour found. Note that for the crossover step, this is probably not too surprising, since the crossover operation itself was implemented in a deterministic way, and only the choice of parents for the crossover was performed randomly.

5.3 Experimental Setup and Results

Parameter	Value
Heuristic	Evolutionary Algorithm
Input	symmetric 50×50 distance matrix
Population size	100
Run time	10,000 iterations
Generators	Mersenne Twister (MT)
	Combination of van der Corput sequences
	and Mersenne Twister:
	M-vdc... : van der Corput sequence
	for mutation/crossover
	R-vdc... : van der Corput seq. for roulette wheel
Seeds per generator	50

Table 5.22: Parameters of Experiment 11.

Experiment 12: Optimizing DeJong's test functions

We also tried to find some connections between the quality of the source of randomness and the result of Genetic Algorithms when optimizing continuous functions. Therefore we applied genetic algorithms on DeJong's test functions. Like in Experiment 6, we chose dimension $k = 20$ for functions f_1, f_3, f_4 and f_5, and dimension $k = 2$ for f_2.

For each of these functions, the population consisted of 50 individuals represented as k-dimensional vectors. Selection was done via the roulette wheel algorithm. For crossover, each component of the offspring vector was chosen randomly from one of the parents. For mutation, we added a Gaussian distributed term to each component. The variance was controlled by a "mutation of mutation rates" approach, i.e. for each individual an additional vector memorized the variance for the mutation step. This additional vector was also mutated, and the corresponding components were copied during the crossover step.

The results of this experiment are shown in Table 5.23, with a representative plot shown in Figure 5.19. Van der Corput sequences again show clearly worse results. But this was expected since all five function had to be optimized in more than one dimension. Function f_2, the only two-dimensional function, could be solved quite well with the Halton sequences. Of the 20-dimensional functions, only f_4 and f_5 could be solved relatively well with the two-dimensional Halton sequence, but with 2 out of 5 cases showing a p-value of 0.05 or below, for

5 Local and population based search heuristics

	f_1	f_2	f_3	f_4	f_5
vdc2 vs. r-512009	×	×	×	×	×
vdc8p1 vs. r-512009	×	×	×	×	×
vdc8p2 vs. r-512009	×	×	×	0.033	×
vdc8p3 vs. r-512009	×	×	×	×	×
vdc8p4 vs. r-512009	×	×	×	×	×
hal2-23 vs. r-512009	×	0.992	×	0.161	0.037
hal2-25 vs. r-512009	×	1	×	0.04	0.367
hal2-35 vs. r-512009	×	0.951	×	0.833	0.023
hal2-37 vs. r-512009	0.216	0.969	×	0.839	0.332
hal2-27 vs. r-512009	×	0.956	×	0.05	0.179
hal20 vs. r-512009	×	0.008	×	0.839	×
r-1009 vs. r-512009	0.677	0.743	0.747	0.839	0.295
r-2003 vs. r-512009	0.166	0.583	0.5	0.839	0.53
r-4001 vs. r-512009	0.812	0.431	0.855	0.839	0.5
r-8009 vs. r-512009	0.529	0.5	0.909	0.839	0.5
r-16001 vs. r-512009	0.54	0.5	0.916	0.5	0.5
r-32003 vs. r-512009	0.395	0.5	0.408	0.5	0.5
r-64007 vs. r-512009	0.5	0.5	0.5	0.5	0.5
r-128021 vs. r-512009	0.5	0.5	0.5	0.5	0.5
r-256019 vs. r-512009	0.5	0.5	0.5	0.5	0.5

Table 5.23: The p-values of the one-sided t test of Experiment 12. Values marked with × were smaller than 0.001. Each generator was compared with the Mersenne Twister via a one-sided t test.

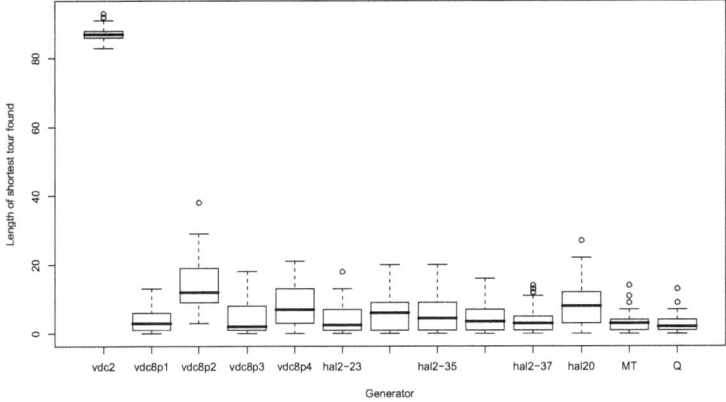

Figure 5.19: Solving DeJong's function f_3 with a genetic algorithm and quasi-random sequences.

each of the two functions. Even the 20-dimensional Halton sequence found significantly worse solutions. The Mersenne Twister with artificially reduced period length had no problem solving any of the five functions. This indicates that using the same random numbers over and over again usually doesn't decrease the quality of the solution obtained from a Genetic Algorithm, as long as the initial sequence is not too regular.

5.3.3 Discussion

For the Simulated Annealing heuristic, the quality of the solution for the Traveling Salesman Problem depended mainly on the period length of the pseudo-random generators we used. The results we received when using simple linear congruential generators were comparable with those we received when using "high end" generators like the Mersenne Twister or numbers from a quantum generator, when we artificially reduced the period lengths of those high-end generators to match those of the LCGs. Even the usage of an explicit polynomial generator led to a result that seemed to only depend on the period length.

5 Local and population based search heuristics

When using quasirandom numbers, Halton sequences of dimension 2 lead to results almost comparable to the results when using a Mersenne Twister or quantum generator, although the results from Halton sequences were slightly worse. Van der Corput sequences however led to drastically inferior results, which shows that sequences that show strong regularities in low dimensions should be avoided in conjunction with Simulated Annealing. For the Traveling Salesman Problem, for example, where the procedure to find a neighbor depends on picking pairs of positions, the pseudorandom generator should at least be able to provide a large number of pairs.

The Genetic Algorithm seemed to be very robust with respect to the quality of the pseudorandom generator we used (see Figure 5.14), with only small deteriorations for linear congruential generators of very small period lengths up to 4000. When using Halton sequences of dimension 2, the solutions did not get worse than when using the quantum generator, when solving the Traveling Salesman Problem. Only the usage of one-dimensional van der Corput sequences led to a decrease in the quality of the solution. Here, the mutation step was identified as the crucial step that depends on good 2-dimensional distribution.

The effects of a source of biased bits had comparable results on both Simulated Annealing as well as the genetic algorithm: For a slight bias up to 0.05, the difference was often not noticeable, while for larger biases, the length of the shortest tour increased heavily.

6 Discussion of theoretical and experimental results

This thesis presents new theoretical results on the effects of using non-perfect random numbers for probabilistic algorithms (Chapters 3 and 4) as well as empirical studies (Chapter 5) that to some extent complement these theoretical studies. We found connections to the error probability, the running time as well as the quality of the solution of algorithms. We will now recapitulate these results and discuss the various notions of randomness that they incorporate.

For the equality test for polynomials, we found that the error probability of its repeated execution is essentially determined by the number of internal states of the pseudorandom generator. This, in turn, is closely related to the Kolmogorov complexity resp. the Shannon entropy of the resulting sequence – the seed of a pseudorandom sequence is an efficient description of the sequence itself. However, this result was only due to the similarity between sequences that stem from different seeds. An alternative approach for creating pseudorandom numbers might eliminate this connection and create numbers that are still not perfectly random but can be used as if they were, at least for that special application.

For Karger's probabilistic algorithm for the minimum cut of a graph, and especially for Schöning's random walk algorithm for the Boolean Satisfiability Problem, our analysis of the new error probability was based on the bias of the random source. The analysis of the latter two algorithms used the fact that the random choices can be divided into two distinct groups, "good choices" and "bad choices". So the quality of the random source seems to be measurable by only distinguishing between these two alternatives. However, the implications of the random numbers might be more subtle: Especially in the scenario of the

6 Discussion of theoretical and experimental results

minimum cut, there might exist a finer notion that even distinguishes between various levels of "good choice". While our analysis is based on a minimum number of edges present in the graph during each step, this number might well depend on the random choices during the run of the algorithm. In other words: some random choices might only eliminate few edges, thus leaving many edges to choose from, while other random choices might eliminate many edges, thus increasing the chance for eliminating the minimum cut. Since this process even depends on the choices made before then, the exact relation is probably very hard to identify.

In addition, note that the theoretical model of the biased sources we considered for the minimum cut and SAT algorithm provide sequences of relatively high Shannon entropy: Since the numbers from these sources are not considered dependent (the probabilities only depend on the given input), the entropy of each number is equal to its conditional entropy (conditioning on the previous numbers), adding to the total entropy of the overall sequence. In the case of the random walk algorithm, the entropy of the total random sequence is even exponential in the size of the input formula. This is more than any reasonably designed pseudorandom generator will generate. But still, no results are known that would show a malevolent influence of a concrete pseudorandom generator on the error probability of any of these two algorithms.

In the case of the randomized QuickSort algorithm, it is somehow obvious that a separation of the random numbers into the categories "good" and "bad" will not lead to a satisfying correlation between randomness and the algorithm's running time. We rather found out that the function

$$g(n) = \left(\sum_{i=1}^{n} p_i H\left(i/n\right)\right)^{-1}$$

shows a connection to the lower bound of QuickSort's running time, which complements the connection to the upper bound shown in List's thesis. Here the probabilities p_i of selecting a pivot element of rank i are weighted with the binary entropy $H(i/n)$ of i/n and summed up. While this term clearly shows a connection to the Shannon entropy, the exact kind of this relation still remains difficult to interpret.

Probabilistic search heuristics, like Simulated Annealing and Genetic Algorithms, are widely used and can be adapted to various situations. However, due to their complexity, they are rather hard to analyze theoretically. In order to collect some knowledge about these techniques, we artificially created sequences of limited randomness. We could then compare the results gained with these artificial sequences with the results gained from "true" random numbers. These numbers were recorded during physical experiments and should, according to quantum physicists, be considered as sequences of independent, uniformly distributed bits. In these experiments, the two heuristics partially showed different behavior when using sequences of varying randomness. For example, limiting the period length of the random source, which essentially simulates a limited number of seeds and thus entropy, had a high influence on Simulated Annealing but almost none on the Genetic Algorithm. Eliminating randomness altogether and using low-discrepancy sets showed a similar result: Simulated Annealing was clearly influenced towards worse solutions, while the Genetic Algorithm showed no difference. On the other hand, introducing a bias to the random sequences influenced both heuristics to about the same degree.

Summarizing, measuring the randomness of a sequence in the context of probabilistic algorithms remains an interesting task. There does not seem to exist a universal measure that can be used to describe the usefulness of a pseudorandom sequence for probabilistic algorithms in general. In the context of probabilistic algorithms, it can be appropriate to measure randomness relative to the problem respectively algorithm it is used for. For example, even sequences of high entropy might cause a probabilistic algorithm to produce sub-optimal results, while other sequences of low entropy might not. Especially when considering concrete implementations of pseudorandom generators, Kolmogorov complexity and its equivalent notions seem inappropriate, since they concentrate on asymptotic behavior rather than concrete, finite objects. Different probabilistic algorithms can vary frequently in the properties of the random numbers they need as well as in the actual amount of randomness. For every probabilistic algorithm, there seems to be an individual notion of what a "typical" random sequence should look like.

6 Discussion of theoretical and experimental results

7 Major results of this thesis

In modern computer science, many problems are solved with the help of probabilistic algorithms. These are often faster than the best known deterministic algorithm for the same problem. Although they often incorporate an error probability, a repeated execution of the algorithm usually decreases that error probability down to a negligible extent.

The analysis of the running time as well as the error probability of a probabilistic algorithm usually presume that the random numbers used by the algorithm are uniformly distributed and independent. However, since computers are deterministic devices, such perfect randomness is difficult to obtain – in order to incorporate "real" randomness, information from outside the computer system must be acquired. Getting such input is slow and therefore used scarcely – generally such numbers are used as a seed for a pseudorandom generator that constructs long sequences from that seed.

This thesis concentrates on the analysis of algorithms with respect to the employment of random sources that do not provide perfect random numbers, like pseudorandom generators or biased sources.

In Chapter 2 we give an overview over the different notions of pseudorandomness and means that are used to measure the amount of randomness of a sequence of numbers. Here we also describe how these notions are used in practice to measure the quality of a source of randomness.

In Chapter 3 we then give new theoretical results for three algorithms that describe implications of using non-perfect random numbers. As a first example, we show that for a basic randomized algorithm for comparing polynomials, repeating the algorithm several times does not always decrease its error probability to the same extent, depending on the pseudorandom generator. We show that

7 Major results of this thesis

for most established types of pseudorandom generators, this decrease mainly depends on the number of possible internal states of that pseudorandom generator, and therefore mainly on the size of the seed. For Karger's probabilistic algorithm for finding the minimum cut of a graph, we show how the algorithm can be adapted to a non-uniform source of randomness. This is shown for the basic version as well as the more sophisticated version with two recursive calls. For the random walk algorithm for the Boolean Satisfiability Problem, we show how a bias from the uniform distribution of the random numbers influences the error probability of the algorithm. The algorithm uses randomness to choose an initial distribution as well as to control the direction of the random walk. We show how both of these steps are influenced by a biased source.

In Chapter 4, we give a lower bound for the number of comparisons in the Randomized Quicksort algorithm, based on the distribution on the choice of the pivot elements. This complements the upper bound given by List in [14]. For both lower and upper bound, we show a connection to the min-entropy of the random source. We also show that the number of bits consumed by the QuickSort algorithm can increase when non-perfect random numbers are used, although the number of pivot elements remains constant.

In the experimental part of this work we examine the impact of various sources of randomness on quality of the solution of probabilistic optimization heuristics. Here we concentrate on Simulated Annealing as a representant for local search heuristics and a genetic algorithm as a representant for population based heuristics. As a reference source of randomness we use bits provided by Prof. Zeilinger's group, gained with the help of a quantum theoretic experiment. These bits are considered uniformly distributed and independent, based on quantum theory. The results of our experiments show that the solution quality of Simulated Annealing can be influenced to a large extent by the period length of the random source. Quasi-random numbers were not suitable, even if their scatter might at first glance look like an advantage. Using k-wise independent random variables did not lead to an improvement over numbers from a linear congruential generator. In contrast, the genetic algorithm was more robust versus the use of sequences with short period length and quasi-random numbers. A bias on the bit level proved to influence both heuristics.

8 Deutsche Zusammenfassung

Viele Problemstellungen werden heutzutage mit probabilistischen Algorithmen gelöst. Diese sind häufig schneller als die besten bekannten deterministischen Verfahren. Die Fehlerwahrscheinlichkeit wird dabei üblicherweise außer Acht gelassen, da eine wiederholte Ausführung des Algorithmus die Fehlerwahrscheinlichkeit rapide sinken lässt.

Sowohl die Analyse der Fehlerwahrscheinlichkeit als auch die Laufzeit-Analyse solcher probabilistischer Algorithmen setzen üblicherweise voraus, dass die benutzten Zufallszahlen gleichverteilt und unabhängig gezogen werden. Da Computer deterministisch sind, ist dies jedoch im Normalfall nur äußerst schwer zu erreichen – um "echten" Zufall einzubinden, muß auf Daten von außen zugegriffen werden. Solche Eingaben sind langsam und werden daher nur sparsam eingesetzt – häufig werden solche Zufallszahlen als Keim für einen Pseudozufallszahlengenerator benutzt, einen Algorithmus, der aus wenigen Zufallszahlen lange Zahlenketten erstellt.

Die vorliegende Arbeit beschäftigt sich mit der Analyse von Algorithmen im Hinblick auf die Verwendung von Zufallsquellen, die keine "perfekten" Zufallszahlen liefern, deren Zufallszahlen also beispielsweise aus einem Pseudozufallszahlengenerator stammen.

Zunächst wird ein Überblick über verschiedene Definitionen von Zufälligkeit gegeben, die vor allem im Bereich der Algorithmik Verwendung finden.

In Kapitel 3 wird für drei Verfahren gezeigt, wie sich das Benutzen nicht-perfekter Zufallszahlen auswirkt. Zunächst wird gezeigt, dass bei einem einfachen Verfahren zum Polynomvergleich durch mehrfaches Wiederholen nicht in jedem Fall die Fehlerwahrscheinlichkeit in gleichem Maße gesenkt wird. Dieser Zusammenhang hängt hauptsächlich von der Anzahl möglicher verschiedener

8 Deutsche Zusammenfassung

interner Zustände des verwendeten Zufallszahlengenerators ab, und damit vor allem von der Größe des Keims. Um einen Effekt wie mit echten Zufallszahlen zu erreichen, dürfen sich die durch verschiedene Keime erzeugten Folgen von Pseudozufallszahlen nicht ähneln. Für Kargers probabilistischen Algorithmus zur Berechnung des minimalen Schnitts eines Graphen wird gezeigt, wie der Algorithmus an eine nicht-gleichverteilte Zufallsquelle angepasst werden kann, ohne dass die Laufzeit in großem Maße ansteigt. Für den Random Walk-Algorithmus für das Erfüllbarkeitsproblem wird gezeigt, wie sich eine Abweichung von der Gleichverteilung bei den im Algorithmus getroffenen Entscheidungen auf die Fehlerwahrscheinlichkeit des Algorithmus auswirkt. Hierbei wird sowohl die Auswirkung auf die initiale Belegung als auch auf die Auswahl der zu ändernden Variablen berücksichtigt.

Für die randomisierte Variante des Sortier-Algorithmus QuickSort wird in Kapitel 4 eine theoretische untere Schranke für die Anzahl der benötigten Vergleiche hergeleitet. Diese untere Schranke wird in Abhängigkeit von den Wahrscheinlichkeiten der Ränge des Pivot-Elements formuliert und zeigt einen Zusammenhang zur Entropie-Funktion. Weiterhin wird gezeigt, dass die Anzahl der vom QuickSort-Algorihmus benötigten Bits bei der Verwendung schlechter Zufallszahlen ansteigt, obwohl sich die Anzahl auszuwählender Pivotelemente nicht ändert.

Im experimentellen Teil dieser Arbeit werden Auswirkungen verschiedener Quellen zufälliger Zahlen auf die Lösungsqualität von probabilistischen Optimierungsverfahren untersucht. Als Repräsentanten von Optimierungsverfahren dienen hier Simulated Annealing als lokale Suchheuristik und ein genetischer Algorithmus als populationsbasierte Suchheuristik. Als Referenz dienen hier Bits, die von Prof. Zeilinger zur Verfügung gestellt wurden und mit Hilfe einer Apparatur erzeugt wurden, die auf Quanteneffekten beruht. Die so gewonnenen Bits werden allgemein als unabhängig und gleichverteilt anerkannt, basierend auf der Quantentheorie. Die Ergebnisse der Experimente zeigen, dass Simulated Annealing äußerst empfindlich auf die Periodenlänge des verwendeten Zufallszahlengenerators reagiert. Quasi-Zufallszahlen scheinen für dieses Verfahren nicht geeignet zu sein, selbst wenn ihre gute Streuung dies zunächst vermuten lässt. Die Verwendung beweisbar k-weiser unabhängiger Zahlen führte zu keiner Verbesserung im Vergleich zu linearen Kongruenzgeneratoren.

Im Gegensatz dazu zeigte sich der genetische Algorithmus robuster gegenüber einer kurzen Periodenlänge und auch gegenüber einer Verwendung von Quasi-Zufallszahlen. Ein Bias auf Bit-Ebene führte bei beiden Verfahren in gleichem Maße zu einer Verschlechterung des Ergebnisses.

8 Deutsche Zusammenfassung

Bibliography

[1] bwGRiD (http://www.bw-grid.de), member of the German D-Grid initiative, funded by the Ministry for Education and Research (Bundesministerium für Bildung und Forschung) and the Ministry for Science, Research and Arts Baden-Württemberg (Ministerium für Wissenschaft, Forschung und Kunst Baden-Württemberg).

[2] Aristotle. *Physics, Translated by R. P. Hardie and R. K. Gaye.* The University of Adelaide Library, 2007.

[3] C. E. Shannon. A mathematical theory of communication. *SIGMOBILE Mob. Comput. Commun. Rev.*, 5(1):3–55, 2001.

[4] Holger H. Hoos and Thomas Stützle. *Stochastic local search: foundations and applications.* Morgan Kaufmann, 2005.

[5] C. A. R. Hoare. Quicksort. *Comput. J.*, 5(1):10–15, 1962.

[6] Beatrice List, Markus Maucher, Uwe Schöning, and Rainer Schuler. Quicksort from an information theoretic view. In Wolfgang Arendt and Wolfgang P. Schleich, editors, *Mathematical Analysis of Evolution, Information, and Complexity*, pages 455 – 464. Wiley-VCH, Berlin, 2009.

[7] Michael O. Rabin. Probabilistic algorithm for testing primality. *J. Number Theory*, 12(1):128–138, 1980.

[8] Manindra Agrawal, Neeral Kayal, and Nitin Saxena. Primes is in P. *Annals of Mathematics*, 160(2):781–793, 2004.

[9] Donald E. Knuth. *Seminumerical Algorithms*, volume 2 of *The Art of Computer Programming*. Addison–Wesley, 1981.

[10] Maya Bar-Hillel and Willem A. Wagenaar. The perception of randomness. *Adv. Appl. Math.*, 12(4):428–454, 1991.

[11] Andreas Futschik. Ist der Euro fair? *Austrian J. Statistics*, 31(1):35–40, 2002.

Bibliography

[12] Howard Karloff and Prabhakar Raghavan. Randomized algorithms and pseudorandom numbers. In *STOC '88: Proceedings of the twentieth annual ACM symposium on Theory of computing*, pages 310–321, New York, NY, USA, 1988. ACM.

[13] Eric Bach. Realistic analysis of some randomized algorithms. *J. Comput. Syst. Sci.*, 42(1):30–53, 1991.

[14] Beatrice List. *Probabilistische Algorithmen und schlechte Zufallszahlen*. PhD thesis, Universität Ulm, 1999.

[15] Mark Matthew Meysenburg. The Effect of Pseudo-Random Number Generator Quality on the Performance of a Simple Genetic Algorithm. Master's thesis, University of Idaho, 1997.

[16] Mark M. Meysenburg and James A. Foster. Randomness and GA performance, revisited. In Wolfgang Banzhaf, Jason Daida, Agoston E. Eiben, Max H. Garzon, Vasant Honavar, Mark Jakiela, and Robert E. Smith, editors, *Proceedings of the Genetic and Evolutionary Computation Conference*, volume 1, pages 425–432, Orlando, Florida, USA, 13-17 July 1999. Morgan Kaufmann.

[17] Dave A. D. Tompkins and Holger H. Hoos. On the quality and quantity of random decisions in stochastic local search for sat. In Luc Lamontagne and Mario Marchand, editors, *Canadian Conference on AI*, volume 4013 of *Lecture Notes in Computer Science*, pages 146–158. Springer, 2006.

[18] Uwe Schöning. *Algorithmik*. Spektrum Akademischer Verlag, 2001.

[19] James L. Massey. Shift-register synthesis and bch decoding. *IEEE Transactions on Information Theory*, 15:122–127, 1969.

[20] Per Martin-Löf. The definition of random sequences. *Information and Control*, 9(6):602–619, 1966.

[21] C.P. Schnorr. Zufälligkeit und Wahrscheinlichkeit. In *Lecture Notes in Mathematics*, volume 218. Springer, 1971.

[22] Oded Goldreich. *Foundations of Cryptography*, volume Basic Tools. Cambridge University Press, 2001.

[23] Michael Luby. *Pseudoranomness and Cryptographic Applications*. Princeton University Press, 1996.

Bibliography

[24] Thomas M. Cover and Joy A. Thomas. *Elements of Information Theory*. Wiley, 1991.

[25] Harald Niederreiter. *Random number generation and quasi-Monte Carlo methods*. Society for Industrial and Applied Mathematics, Philadelphia, PA, USA, 1992.

[26] The MathWorks – MATLAB and Simulink for Technical Computing, http://www.mathworks.com/.

[27] Heiko Bauke and Stephan Mertens. Pseudo random coins show more heads than tails. *J.STAT.PHYS.*, 114:1149, 2004.

[28] Makoto Matsumoto and Takuji Nishimura. Mersenne twister: a 623-dimensionally equidistributed uniform pseudo-random number generator. *ACM Trans. Model. Comput. Simul.*, 8(1):3–30, January 1998.

[29] The R Project for Statistical Computing, http://www.r-project.org/.

[30] Maple, www.maplesoft.com.

[31] C. De Canniere and B. Preneel. Trivium specifications. *eSTREAM, ECRYPT Stream Cipher Project*, 2006.

[32] Personal correspondence with A. Zeilinger and T. Jennewein, University of Vienna.

[33] T. Jennewein, U. Achleitner, G. Weihs, H. Weinfurter, and A. Zeilinger. A fast and compact quantum random number generator. *Review of Scientific Instruments*, 71:1675–1680, April 2000.

[34] L. H. C. (Leonard Henry Caleb) Tippett. *Random sampling numbers*, volume 15 of *Tracts for computers*. Cambridge University Press, Cambridge, UK, 1927. Reprinted in 1952. Reprinted in 1959 with a foreword by Karl Pearson.

[35] The Marsaglia Random Number CDROM including the Diehard Battery of Tests of Randomness, http://stat.fsu.edu/pub/diehard/.

[36] RANDOM.ORG – True Random Number Service, http://random.org/.

[37] Christos H. Papadimitriou. *Computational Complexity*. Addison Wesley, November 1993.

[38] Miklos Santha and Umesh V. Vazirani. Generating quasi-random sequences from semi-random sources. *J. Comput. Syst. Sci.*, 33(1):75–87, August 1986.

Bibliography

[39] N. Alon and M. O. Rabin. Biased coins and randomized algorithms. In F.P. Preparata and S. Micali, editors, *Advances in Computing Research*, volume 5, pages 499–507. JAI Press, 1989.

[40] Beatrice List, Markus Maucher, Uwe Schöning, and Rainer Schuler. Randomized quicksort and the entropy of the random source. In Lusheng Wang, editor, *11th Annual International Computing and Combinatorics Conference (COCOON 2005)*, pages 450–460, 2005.

[41] Markus Maucher, Uwe Schöning, and Hans A. Kestler. An empirical assessment of local and population based search methods with different degrees of pseudorandomness. Technical report, Universität Ulm, June 2008.

[42] Benny Chor and Oded Goldreich. On the power of two-point based sampling. *Journal of Complexity*, 5(1):96–106, 1989.

[43] Michael Luby and Avi Wigderson. Pairwise independence and derandomization. Technical Report CSD-95-880, 1995.

[44] D. H. Lehmer. Computer technology applied to the theory of numbers. In *Studies in Number Theory*, pages 117–151. Prentice-Hall, 1969.

[45] D. Shanks. Five number-theoretic algorithms. In *Proceedings of the Second Manitoba Conference on Numerical Mathematics*, pages 51–70, 1972.

[46] L. Adleman, K. Manders, and G. Miller. On taking roots in finite fields. In *Proc.18th Annual IEEE Symp. Foundations of Computer Sciences*, pages 175–178, 1977.

[47] Gary L. Miller. Riemann's hypothesis and tests for primality. *Journal of Computer and System Sciences*, 13:300–317, December 1976. invited publication.

[48] Yossi Azar, Andrei Z. Broder, Anna R. Karlin, Nathan Linial, and Steven Phillips. Biased random walks. *Combinatorica*, 16(1):1–18, 1996.

[49] Michael Mitzenmacher and Eli Upfal. *Probability and Computing: Randomized Algorithms and Probabilistic Analysis*. Cambridge University Press, New York, NY, USA, 2005.

[50] Howard J. Karloff and Prabhakar Raghavan. Randomized algorithms and pseudorandom numbers. *Journal of the ACM (JACM)*, 40(3):454–476, 1993.

[51] David R. Karger. Global min-cuts in $\mathcal{RNC}$, and other ramifications of a simple min-cut algorithm. *Proceedings of the Fourth Annual ACM-SIAM Symposium on Discrete Algorithms*, pages 21–30, 1993.

[52] Stephen A. Cook. The complexity of theorem-proving procedures. In *STOC '71: Proceedings of the third annual ACM symposium on Theory of computing*, pages 151–158, New York, NY, USA, 1971. ACM.

[53] U. Schöning. A probabilistic algorithm for k-sat based on limited local search and restart. *Algorithmica*, 32:615–623, 2002.

[54] Donald E. Knuth. *Sorting and Searching*, volume 3 of *The Art of Computer Programming*. Addison–Wesley, 1973.

[55] Martin Tompa. Lecture notes on probabilistic algorithms and pseudorandom generators. Technical report, University of Washington, July 1991.

[56] R. Sedgewick and P. Flajolet. *Analysis of Algorithms*. Addison–Wesley, 1996.

[57] Beatrice List, Markus Maucher, Uwe Schöning, and Rainer Schuler. Quick-Sort from an information theoretic view. Wolfgang Arendt, Wolfgang Schleich (eds.), Mathematical analysis of evolution, information, and complexity. Wiley-VCH. 455-464, 2009.

[58] S. Kirkpatrick, C. D. Gelatt, and M. P. Vecchi. Optimization by simulated annealing. *Science, Number 4598, 13 May 1983*, 220, 4598:671–680, 1983.

[59] Nicholas Metropolis, Arianna W. Rosenbluth, Marshall N. Rosenbluth, Augusta H. Teller, and Edward Teller. Equation of state calculations by fast computing machines. *The Journal of Chemical Physics*, 21(6):1087–1092, 1953.

[60] S. Geman and D. Geman. Stochastic relaxation, Gibbs distributions, and the Bayesian restoration of images. *IEEE Transactions on Pattern Analysis and Machine Intelligence*, 6:721–741, 1984.

[61] John H. Holland. *Adaptation in Natural and Artificial Systems*. University of Michigan Press, 1975.

[62] K. Mathias and D. Whitley. Genetic operators, the fitness landscape and the traveling salesman problem. In *Parallel Problem Solving from Nature*, pages 219–228. Elsevier Science Publishers, 1992.

[63] Gerhard Reinelt. *The Traveling Salesman*. Springer Berlin Heidelberg, 1994.

Bibliography

[64] K.A. DeJong. *An Analysis of the Behavior of a Class of Genetic Adaptive Systems*. PhD thesis, Dept. of Electrical Eng. and Computer Science, Univ. of Michigan, 1975.

[65] J. B. Kruskal. Extremely portable random number generator. *Commun. ACM*, 12(2):93–94, 1969.

[66] K. Mulmuley. *Computational Geometry: An Introduction through Randomized Algorithms*. Prentice-Hall, 1994.

[67] Uwe Schöning. *Algorithmen - kurz gefasst*. Spektrum Akademischer Verlag, 1997.

[68] Jozef Gruska. *Foundations of Computing*. International Thomson Computer Press, 1997.

[69] Ming Li and Paul M. B. Vitanyi. *An Introduction to Kolmogorov Complexity and Its Applications*. Springer-Verlag, Berlin, 1993.

Index

δ-random source, 38

Aristotle, 1

beam splitter, 36
bias, 100
bits, 99
Boolean Satisfiability Problem, 53
bounded entropy, 73
box plot, 96
BucketSort, 65

compressibility, 19
crossover, 86

DeJong's test functions, 92, 108
Deutsche Zusammenfassung, 133
Diehard sequence, 37
discrepancy, 31
Divide and Conquer, 66

Entropy, 28, 70
entropy, 28
equality of polynomials, 43
evolutionary algorithm, 87
experimental setup, 92

geometric distribution, 77
graph, 8

Halton sequences, 103

Hoare, C.A.R., 65

independence, 32

k-wise independence, 32
Karger, 48
Kolmogorov complexity, 19

Landau's notation, 8
local optimum, 94
lower bound, 75

major results, 131
Markov chain, 12, 85
Martin Löf randomness, 21
martingale, 26
Median-of-three QuickSort, 71
Mersenne Twister, 35
Metropolis-Hastings algorithm, 84
min-entropy, 75
minimum cut, 48
Monte Carlo, 30
multiset, 7
mutation, 86

noise, 94

pairwise independence, 32
period length, 96
population based heuristics, 86

Index

predictability, 26
pseudorandom generator, 32
Pseudorandom number generator, 67

quantum effects, 36
quasi-random sequences, 30, 103
QuickSort, 65

Random QuickSort, 67
random.org, 38

SAT, 53
Schema Theorem, 88, 89
search heuristics, 84
selection, 86
Simulated Annealing, 84, 96
slightly random source, 38
Sorting, 66
statistical test, 21

upper bound, 74

van der Corput sequences, 103

Die VDM Verlagsservicegesellschaft sucht für wissenschaftliche Verlage abgeschlossene und herausragende

Dissertationen, Habilitationen, Diplomarbeiten, Master Theses, Magisterarbeiten usw.

für die kostenlose Publikation als Fachbuch.

Sie verfügen über eine Arbeit, die hohen inhaltlichen und formalen Ansprüchen genügt, und haben Interesse an einer honorarvergüteten Publikation?

Dann senden Sie bitte erste Informationen über sich und Ihre Arbeit per Email an *info@vdm-vsg.de*.

Sie erhalten kurzfristig unser Feedback!

VDM Verlagsservicegesellschaft mbH
Dudweiler Landstr. 99　　　　　　　Telefon +49 681 3720 174
D - 66123 Saarbrücken　　　　　　　Fax　　　+49 681 3720 1749
www.vdm-vsg.de

Die VDM Verlagsservicegesellschaft mbH vertritt

Printed by Books on Demand GmbH, Norderstedt / Germany